D0242754

# THE SKY SUSPENDED

## A FIGHTER PILOT'S STORY

## JIM BAILEY

BLOOMSBURY

First published in 1964 under the title *Eskimo Nel*

This new edition first published in Great Britain in 1990
This paperback edition published 2005

Bloomsbury Publishing Plc, 38 Soho Square, London W1D 3HB

A CIP catalogue record for this book
is available from The British Library

ISBN 0 7475 7773 0

10 9 8 7 6 5 4 3 2

All papers used by Bloomsbury Publishing are natural,
recyclable products made from wood grown in well-managed forests.
The manufacturing processes conform to the
environmental regulations of the country of origin.

PICTURE SOURCES
Flight-Lieutenant Holloway: pages 6 and 7
Keystone Press Agency: page 8
Popperfoto: page 4

Photoset by Rowland Phototypesetting Limited, Bury St Edmunds, Suffolk
Printed by Clays Ltd, St Ives plc

www.bloomsbury.com

# CONTENTS

# FOREWORD

Dear Jim,

Your telephone call, after all these twenty-three years that we have neither seen nor spoken to one another, made me very happy. You have asked me to write a foreword to your book and this has sent me groping back into the past, trying to discover some impression which would touch off a train of thought.

The coincidence is apt, for you write from South Africa and this concerns the Wildebeest, not that ugly brute of the Kruger Park, but one of my favourite aeroplanes, an ancient, square-rigged biplane, full of loyalty and character. In its cockpit was a notice, long-winded by jet standards, but what did it matter then, we were in no hurry. It said, very firmly, 'This aircraft is not to be flown at a speed in excess of 140 mph.'

At that time I was twenty-one and though I had five years advance on you we both belonged, as concerns flying, to the bird-age, in time to be superseded by the jet-age. We were known as birdmen, sometimes even intrepid birdmen. But our pleasure did not lie in this kind of hollow flattery. It lay, as you have so beautifully depicted in your book – at least for those whose senses were alive – in the joy brought to us by naked contact with the air, our natural element, with the brutal buffeting of the slipstream, with the passionate feel of speed; feel, I say, for in an open cockpit at 100 mph, as on the back of a galloping horse, speed, clean and breath-taking, is realistic, not motionless and pressurised, as in a Boeing. I remember how reluctant we were, when we relinquished our trim little pre-war Furies for the all-powerful Hurricanes and Spitfires, to close the hood and shut ourselves off from the element to which we belonged. At least we were able to re-open them – but the age of the hermetically-sealed jet was not far off.

This transitional period was the one in which we came to know one another, you a 'wandering scholar', I a professional airman, a 'regular' with an irregularity of conduct and character which doomed me already for high office. There happened to be a war on (as they used to say airily) and this gave intense drama to the decor: the obligation to face up squarely to death; the hope one nurtured, but dared not openly express, of survival. The terror of others, who were naïve enough not to hide it, believing you were less terrified than they. But there were compensations in which much beauty lay, though some of it was gashed with hideous high-lights.

There were those dawn patrols when we pierced the low-lying mist to meet the rising sun; there was the exquisite solitude of those patrols miles high in the black of night, when only reason's domination over unreason prevented an occasional urge to end it all with a deliberate insane plunge into the dark chasm, miles deep, below. There was the fearful, sweating apprehension of having to fly into the massed cohorts of the enemy, happily allayed at one's first encounter by the realisation that they could not all round on you and devour you at once. Quite the contrary, it was us, the nimble, fleet-footed fighters who usually had the advantage. But only on condition that we never, for a moment, relaxed our guard, nor made a fatal error. I remember that evening when the high haze was infused with the crimson of the setting sun: we were jumped by three Messerschmitt 109s. I can still see the square wing-tips and black crosses of the one that should have got me as it flashed across just above. I had already whipped into a turn on the warning cry from the tail look-out – it was the Ace. But a few wing-spans to starboard Hamilton's aircraft was rolling over, wrapped in flame and dipping towards the earth five miles below.

His was a swifter end than the slow death of Gordon of which you were a sad and helpless witness. You think that the swift deaths were easier than the ugly, drawn-out ones. It is not a point I should care to argue, but on the two occasions when I had to bale out I remember above all the extraordinary calm which possessed me when the issue, life or death, still remained to be decided. The first time I found time for a brief but homely chat with ground control; the second time, when an Me 110 made a proper mess of my aircraft and me, I heard myself mutter, 'Christ . . .' but in a hushed voice, so that the ladies would not hear, as if I had spilled some tea on the drawing-room carpet. I believe it to be true, I pray so anyway, that some unseen peace, given from a source beyond us, possesses us, be we saint or criminal, when we face a head-on encounter with death.

Let us be honest – we felt satisfaction in the destruction of an enemy. More often than not there was a rare, dramatic beauty in the sight of an aircraft, even one of ours, on its last, headlong swoop towards earth, or a watery tomb. There was the thrill of the chase, more gloriously stimulating, let's admit, than any notion of defending the last barriers of the free world. Finally there was the simple contentment that any professional feels in a job well done.

All this seemed mundane enough, but terrible reactions, which we even managed to hold in check long after they made themselves felt, were building up in our minds and bodies. Sooner or later came the moment when we, the surviving witnesses of this gay, sporting carnage, had had our fill; and fatigue, with its by-products fear and revolt, blunted or destroyed our natural (or should we say professional?) impulses. And we became infected instead with a morbid terror of dying, filled with the same of killing, saddened with the endless departure of friends to their lone home, repulsed by the futile, boasting claims of the wiping-out, the annihilation of the enemy. Lauded as heroes, hung with medals, we only longed to withdraw into the mountains – or the marshes – there 'to forget yesterday and tomorrow'.

Luckily for you and me, and others of our ilk, we were still living in the romantic age of flying, and were thus deeply affected by the influences, supernatural at times, sensual at others, of our chosen element, the air. (The bourgeois jet-age has insulated airmen from their element, though I think no less of them, for the host of convenient miracles they perform.)

Which brings me to the point in your thinking, a point upon which we have a common homing no matter from where we start in time or space. It is now twenty-three years after, but I sensed it at the time: you had plumbed the depths, you had comprehended that flying was more than just a profession. It was an art, a super-terrestrial desire, a seventh heaven. I could never have become a pilot had I not felt a veritable passion, at the tender age of fourteen, for flying. (That you were originally seduced by the gastronomic possibilities of the Oxford Squadron is just as valid, in view of the use you made of them.)

To return to me: I watched, with envy and amazement, the Siskins from North Weald as they gambolled, streaks of silver in the sunny sky. I felt a solemn thrill as I was allowed to climb into the cockpit of the Supermarine S.6. which later won the Schneider Trophy, of the Westland aircraft which flew over Mount Everest. I carved them out from wood, despising ready-made models. At eighteen I flew my first solo and chose, among fifty other subjects, to write a thesis on Bird Flight for my passing-out examination. (The great Whittle, not so long before, had delivered his historic thesis on gas-turbines.) The gay aerobatics of the plover; the soaring flight of the buzzards above my native Quantock Hills; the adroit mallard, victim of high wing-loading, with his power take-off and skilful, if panicky, landing; the ponderous but graceful airmanship of the swan – all this filled my world, a world full of bird-flight and bird-song, of changing seasons and skies, of long walks over the hills, with the scent of heather and the drone of bees and the soft feel of wet peat beneath my feet, the feel in my legs and lungs of the power needed to climb and the effortless gain of speed in the descent.

All this, and the war too, naturally sent my thoughts wandering on the final outcome. Nature provided the decor, war was the theme. It is impossible not to compare one's own lot with that of others. My escape, in which Hamilton was killed, was just one; another was like yours, when you thought Hardie called 'I'm wounded'. Having no Hardie the first warning I had was a bullet which, having pierced my radio, passed between my legs and shattered in the cockpit. Three Me 109s were queuing up behind me. Another was the Dornier's cannon-shell which exploded in the cockpit and resulted in an early morning swim in the North Sea; another was a head-on meeting with an Me 110, a shattered windscreen, a drenching in petrol, no fire, but a toe blown off (as you unheroically put it); and so on, like you, with heaven knows how many times, the wings, the fuselage and the propeller riddled with bullets. Modesty forbids us to go into the hazards of ice, fog, radio failures, and a total blackout at night.

One is tempted to ask: why should I have escaped the ultimate, the classic fate – a charred corpse, a wet grave on the ocean-bed, a mutilated body? One is further tempted to look for an answer. But you say, 'In a hundred years time I do not suppose it will make two hoots of difference what we have done, or thought or said.' At all events, I do not think we need worry; posterity will no doubt decide.

I have said enough; but I want once more to quote you. 'Airmen,' you say, 'with many tales to tell, are mostly mute.' You are right. The best airmen are mostly simple people, who have been so overwhelmed by their love for flying that it has driven some of them to drink, others to silence, as great love often does. But occasionally there arises one, a poet, a philosopher, who succeeds in lending coherent reason to their love. This you have certainly done for me and, I believe, for every airman of our age who, reading your book, will feel you have given wings to his inmost thoughts.

PETER TOWNSEND

P.S. I am glad to hear that you too had trouble with your knees knocking together. Mine used sometimes to shake so violently up and down on the rudder bar that I had to hold them down with my hand.

P.T.

# PREFACE

I have a feeling – no, more than that, a presentiment – that when we eventually and in the fullness of time go to heaven we travel not singly but in groups. After death, we would wait for those who are nearest to us in affection, and then move off together. This could lead to surprising associations; for a mother will have persuaded herself that she was close to her husband, or to her daughter, yet she finds herself voyaging to heaven, not with them, but with her baker, and at that, the baker is not a part of her family but she has become part of his. As you take on a cook or a baker, remember this risk.

When Roman mercenaries fought each other during the Roman elections, they used first to greet their enemy with a 'Salve'. I do not doubt that when Christian and Muslim killed each other on the edges of Europe, there will have been many occasions when the slaughtered of both sides picked each other up and moved off happily together. During this last war who is to suppose that this was not sometimes the case?

# Chapter 1

# Why War?

Having been born in October 1919, it has always seemed to me that I was called into this world as a result of the junketing which followed upon the Armistice. And things being what they were, I was ripe for the Second World War, when I was called upon by special letter, dated September 2nd, 1939 at the mature age of 19 years and 10 months.

If then this book searches into this experience, I have had good cause to be curious. Time was when Europeans accepted the whole silly military process, with its medals, its whinnying generals and its skewered peasants, questionless and unhesitatingly. Mercifully those days pass.

To glance at the last ten centuries of Europe's warfaring reveals that precious little has been achieved by it beyond the dissipation of Europe's wealth, like the burning of coffee or the tipping of milk into the sea. How many fine men have been butchered in search of ends which were negligible! For the nations and languages are such as they were and I cannot for the life of me see how anyone would have been bettered if English had replaced the French language or if French had overtaken English. It would merely have made foreign travel for the victorious nation a shade more expensive. Only a poet can take and hold a country. By how many centuries might we not be ahead in discovery, if we had not wasted our substance on this purposeless slaughter.

But to my story.

To some extent England resembles St Kilda's. Her people,

like puffins and shearwaters, leave home once they are fledged, to disappear over the ocean boundary. Some do not return; some return to die; many, when the time comes to breed, go back to rear their children and to teach them in those sea-bound rookeries their own prejudices before these children in their turn disappear over the horizon to distant and warmer lands. So it was with my forbears.

My grandfather emigrated from Keighley, in Yorkshire; and my father was born and bred in the Eastern Province of South Africa. He himself dropped his first brood in Africa and then, taking unto himself an Irish wife, dropped his next brood in England where I was born, reared and educated until the war.

Wars coming, it is wise, where possible, to enjoy them. Of personal detail much is forgotten. The faces and names even of my closest friends have faded like a vapour trail. Acquaintances, youthful tipplers, pilots who spend two cheerful nights on the aerodrome and then were sped, lads whom I well loved — forgotten long ago. Time works on the memory like sea on the body. The currents wash up after a month little of that which at one time existed. They were reported missing; their effects were returned; doubtless someone else took their place, that is all. And if the flesh is parted, scenery and cloud effects have gone further. But yet, but yet the past is not always irretrievable. The whine of an engine, the smell of an exhaust, sparks flying back from an exhaust, memory is jogged and the details spring vividly to life.

# Chapter 2

# My Country Background

The early call-up caught me. For I had flown in the Oxford University Air Squadron before the war, along with Richard Hillary and his friends. It had been the only contribution which I could make at my age to peace. In addition, I had rejoined the squadron because two South African friends had led me to believe that it served the best food in Oxford. One of them was later killed over London, the other, Andrew Duncan, over Tobruk.

It was a perfect year, that year before the storm broke. I was possessed of an 'hydroptic, immoderate thirst for human learning', and by the great feast that was the university, delighted. I enjoyed an equal passion for country sports – polo in the summer, pike-fishing and game shooting in the winter – so that it occurred to me that I was close to that bliss for which the faithful must wait their lifetime.

Truly, happiness is infectious. I would care to be able to fasten onto paper all that joy. I believe now that I was too backward and naive properly to benefit by the university, but the eminent economist Roy Harrod taught me economics, removing his coat and scratching his pits during tutorials – that, in sum, is all I remember of them. Gilbert Ryle imbued me with philosophy. 'What exactly is philosophy?' I enquired of him one quiet summer morning, gazing out over the Gothic quadrangle. I jotted down his reply: 'That is a very interesting question and one which philosophers are just beginning to ask themselves.'

My sporting companion, and the man who above all others had brought me up, was our gamekeeper, Alan Howe. Since, with a boy's affection, I felt a greater affinity for animals and plants than for people, I required no more human friendship than his own. He was the sort of Englishman who thinks for himself, which is the characteristic of the countryman, of the man whose opinions have not been formed for him by his newspaper and radio. 'They cannot expect the unemployed to fight – for they have nothing to fight for.' 'I tell you, Master Jim, that in the old days the labourer was better off; he took less money but it bought more. He kept his own pig, etc, etc.' Alan Howe had had a part in the previous war, which provided him with his own occasion for adventure and foreign travel; so that although he disapproved of war, he often chatted about it. On his way to the campaign in East Africa, he stopped off in Durban, which word he was accustomed to accent on the last syllable, Durbàn. His father had been the gamekeeper on Bletchington Estate before him. 'He had a stroke while handling the ferrets; when they found his body, the ferrets had eaten part of his face away. He used to make us boys climb an elm to put a trap for kestrels in the old crow's nest there. The trunk at the summit of the giant elm, as I remember it, hung back quite a bit. It was smooth where the squirrels had run along it . . .' Howe had his favourite phrases. My brother and I would ask him a stupid question: 'Mr Howe, do you know your nose is crooked?' and he would put the tweed hat on the back of his head – 'Is it be godly?'

It was thus a year of magic. I did not take much part in university life; I had little time or inclination to do so. But an athletic friend who studied agriculture, Jamie, a fine Scot, shared rooms with me and I thus tasted more of the university fellowship and felt less lonely there than I might otherwise have done. There was a group of us who met to discuss the simplest and most junior questions in philosophy, such as: 'When is it right to revolt?' 'What is meant by the State?' 'If a man is outside the contract and has no vote, must he obey the law?' – questions which have left the class-room and now exercise us in contemporary politics. I enjoyed all this; I endeavoured to convert my friends to determinism; indeed, had the war not come, I should have been compelled the following year to attempt a counter-reformation. There were warm summer nights in the college garden; evenings frittered away playing bowls while the sky darkened or, with a glass of port, discussing, in the fashion of undergraduates, all topics under the sun.

I played a season of polo that delectable summer. The polo ground was in Kirtlington Park, about three miles from our home in Bletchington. On a warm summer afternoon I could canter across two parks to the polo ground, to practise with stick and ball against the coming week-end. June in Oxfordshire is knee-deep in grass; where there were glades in it, as on the shorn polo ground, pairs of English partridges would be sunning themselves. Chiff-chaffs, willow-wren, woodlark, blackcap would be singing and from the dense oak and chestnut foliage, young rooks would take off and make their short, tailless flights from tree to tree. Such a summer is all birdsong.

Most of us knew at the same time that a war with Germany menaced us. My robust, one-legged father, Abe Bailey, had denounced it over three successive summers. He had been a loyal friend to Winston Churchill in his darker days and shared the same clear-cut views on the nature of resurgent Germany. For years the unemployed had been drifting across England in search of work that was not obtainable, and for years the Nazis had been arming. My eldest brother had dined with Sir John Simon in the spring of 1939 and had put to him that war with Germany was inevitable. 'My dear Sir,' replied Sir John, 'you are an alarmist.' Most of my undergraduate friends did no work that summer term, in the belief that if war was brewing, they should not waste their time. The harvest was near. My father, whom I was never to see again and who would never again see his family, sailed to South Africa. Alan Howe and I discussed the probability of war; talk that brought to the pit of my stomach the same queasy sensations as when I had waited, at school, to be beaten. On September 2nd the Germans invaded Poland.

These two German wars have profoundly altered the countries concerned. My father finely portrayed one of the best types of the old order. He was a self-made man, deserving that soubriquet because he refused any sort of assistance from his own pa. Father and son stood up as headstrong, self-reliant individualists. Abe ran away from home in Queenstown at the age of eight because he could stomach his own father no longer and later went to the goldfields in Barberton in preference to a university. He made and lost several fortunes. His description of the early days and the man who made good, was: 'Get on, Get on, Get Honest.'

The parched and ever-stretching plains of South Africa were earlier peopled by Bushmen, the tiny, stone-age hunters among the vast herds of buck. Cattle-raising Hottentots came along the coast and lodged with their heavy, long-horned cattle. Then, over a period of a thousand years, African war-bands had moved down from the north, the Ovambos and Hereros down the west coast, the Tswana-speaking people in the centre, the Zulus and Xhosas to the east. Chaka held Natal and later Moselekatse the Transvaal. The Dutch colonised the Cape in the 17th century and then, during the 18th and 19th centuries spread outward and up-country in many a long and adventurous trek. These were all pastoral or agricultural people. With the discovery of gold a new type of man appeared, English, Jew and German. Fighting and struggling in the pioneer days, they changed a primitive country over forty miraculous years into a modern industrial state. In the van of this movement was my father.

He would turn up in England in time for the Derby and leave after the pheasant shooting. His face would be tanned a deep mahogany by the South African sun. He would pinch the cheeks of his children, present them with bright red apples, clench and unclench his powerful fists. Thenceforward would commence a long series of lunches and dinners to which he invited friends, rich and famous. He hectored his guests, made terrible puns, repeated the same anecdotes over and over again, laughed largely each time, spent lavishly and enjoyed every penny he spent. What he touched, flourished, for he possessed imagination. He gave generously, was mightily susceptible to flattery, adored titles. He was a great patriot, loving both South Africa and Britain like a just polygamist with two wives. I think he never went to any other country.

Deeply as I feared war at that time, I cannot pretend that I looked upon its outbreak through and through as a disaster. A few days before Lord Amery had compelled Neville Chamberlain to stand his ground, I had sat down in front of my bookshelves, to enquire of myself why I had read so widely. For the first time I fully realised that I was baffled by the notion of purpose; by the fact that, of all the people I knew, their minor day-to-day actions were significant. But when I came to ask about their major, lifelong aims no one could answer me convincingly. So I had turned to the classics and to authors famous for their wisdom to guide me or to drop some sort of a hint to me. But so I made the adolescent, yet startling, appreciation that although each detail of the adult's life holds some sort of a goal, the whole is purposeless. And various systems of importance, convention and ceremony were used to conceal this hard truth from themselves. Books, therefore, could not help. With an impatience that was physical as well as mental, I used of nights to walk the city of Oxford and I had reached a stage where it seemed imperative to me that I should gain some practical experience in addition to book-learning, and acquire a little more knowledge about real life, about flesh and blood with which to match my boy's studies, when war broke. I did not welcome war; I feared it then as today I hate it. Yet it had something to offer me and when it came, I sought to profit by it as richly as I might.

One night that summer, I was dozing in my tent at our Reserve Flying Camp. Two voices in the next tent were droning away, discussing this and that, when they touched on the subject of myself. The one voice, belonging to a contemporary who has since been a Cabinet Minister, said: 'He is a queer sort of chap.' His companion added: 'He looks only sixteen.'

# Chapter 3

# RAF Training

I used to reckon that I was the only pilot upon either side whose mother throughout the war had more flying hours to her credit than her son. For my mother had taken upon herself to pioneer women's aviation and to attempt record-breaking flights to South Africa, flying solo in a De Havilland Moth. This helped to focus attention upon the air-routes which Imperial Airways commenced soon after this. Just before she set off on her second attempt, she drew me, a school-kid, to one side and asked me how she should handle logarithms. I told her that I was doing them next term. Nevertheless, undaunted, we knelt down onto the deep-piled drawing-room carpet with a sheet of paper and attempted a few misty speculations into the nature of trigo-nometry. On this occasion, she was lost in the Sahara four days. At other times, she had force-landed in Spain and Russia. Indeed, the circle of her mishaps might have been ever-widening had she not walked into a propeller when it was spinning. This curtailed her valiant activities for a while before she could come back again to flying.

So my papers obliged me to report at the RAF Volunteer Reserve Centre of Oxford City. I stood in a queue. The queue moved slowly. I chatted with John Ruckeene, the slight, dark son of a bluff admiral of nine children who lived next door to ourselves. John and two of his brothers were soon to be killed. We bemoaned the war, idly speculating on what the unhappy future might hold for us. My neighbour in the queue next ahead of me joined us in the conversation. 'It is better than clerking anyway,' he drummed into me. Light broke then; for I was to discover in the following years that many men without my opportunities fought chiefly for enjoyment. Life in the industrial cities of Europe moved in so church-going, petty and poor a manner, was in itself so intellectually, legally and sexually restricted, the cannonade provided many a young man with a welcome change. When I eventually reached the head of the queue they paid me a paltry sum and told me to be home again. They repeated this each week for six weeks. I grew impatient. Alan Howe wisely counselled me that I would have had sufficient before it was all over.

In due time, a posting came through to the initial training wing at Cambridge. We marched about the town behind the tall amateur boxer, the Lord Douglas-Hamilton, blowing on his bagpipes. An interesting argument developed there; some among us held that no man should attempt to decide his fate; he should volunteer for nothing, avoid nothing. The other school of thought, of which I was in those days a protagonist, urged that one should choose and then single-mindedly pursue that choice. Whichever way we voted, however, the squad of us were sent off to Hastings and parcelled out among the seaside lodging houses, on whose landladies we were billeted.

Poor landladies! You were never hardened to this sort of boarder! Until that day my approach to old ladies had been that of the god-fearing Hindu. For I had judged them to be an unnecessary encumbrance to society, believing that the world had been better off if they were to be put upon the pyres of their husbands, tidily, like Hindu widows. Now I was to learn better.

The drawing-room of our boarding house was divided into two by a curtain; upon the one side lived the usual boarding-house clientele of widows and spinsters, upon the other the young and lusty air-crew. It was the curtain which deceived us; for it led both groups to believe that they were in a different room and that their conversation was inaudible to the party next door; whereas, when I sat by myself in the sitting-room, I could hear every word these good women let fall. Indeed, they were charitable enough about us but I do not care to think in what unfeeling phrases they must have heard themselves described. They dwelt in a world, it seemed, where you loved without often being loved; where you were all kindness and light but yet you lacked the power to help. If one of them should receive a letter, it must be read aloud and her friends shuffled in after breakfast to hear it. 'This is from my niece, you know, the one I was speaking about yesterday.' Then, perhaps, one of my companions would stride into his part of the room, expressing his opinion of the breakfast in sufficient bawdy, so that the letter-reader would probably have to pause in her reading until she could make herself heard again. In this way, that curtain really brought us together.

When we lined up on the parade for our daily march – shortest on the right, tallest on the left – I used to look down our ranks and think of us as so many geese fattening for market. I do not know to this day whether the others thought similarly and looked at me as at a goose – I expect it was.

Before Christmas, along with a group of friends, I was posted to Cranwell, the principal RAF College, in Lincolnshire. On December 30th we arrived there. Our training aircraft were Harts and Hinds, biplanes that were vintage but withal a delight to fly. My instructor was an ill-tempered Rhodesian, Flying Officer Chater, who nevertheless was a first-class teacher, demanding, though not receiving, absolute precision in the handling of his aircraft. I believe that I, at first a gastronomic pilot only, owe my life to this exactness.

We were chiefly undergraduates, on this the second war-course at Cranwell. When they divided us into those who would fly single-engined aircraft and those to fly twins, I applied for single-engined aircraft. I had hoped to become a fighter pilot for I was of too independent a nature, I feared, to belong to a larger crew and too fastidious to bomb civilians. In the event, the bomber pilots of our course were almost all killed or made prisoner in the early stages of the war; all, that is, except for a very tall law student with a receding chin, Peter Barlowe. He was landy and vague, so tall, in truth, that he could not squeeze under the perspex canopy of a fighter. He walked with his hands clasped behind his back. He survived all the athletes and the lean, natural pilots, who died early. I met him in Oakham after he had completed two tours of operations. Mutual friends told me that when he returned a salute, it was as if he were flicking a fly off his ear. He remained the same vague, good-natured chap, to all appearances, wholly impractical. When some friends told him a dirty story, he would chuckle for hours, repeating the story to himself and laughing so whole-heartedly, I felt he was on each occasion getting the point of it for the first time. He introduced me to a cocktail known as 'Hudson's Breath', and then proceeded to describe how one of his colleagues, who always came home with engine trouble before making his target, was known as 'Boomerang Thomson'. After his period of rest, Peter went back to a third tour of operational flying and was killed then.

Unexpectedly, the fighter pilots among us enjoyed better fortune. Pat Dawley, a Welshman, was killed with the army but David Scott-Malden, an immensely talented contemporary at Winchester, after two years commanded the Norwegian squadron and led the Hornchurch fighter-wing. Diabetes later compelled him to drop operational flying. Thomas Lund was a brown-haired, gentle, other-worldly student of medieval history, who ought never to have been flying at all. Nevertheless, he succeeded in maintaining an exact balance between the German aircraft he destroyed and the RAF fighters he absentmindedly wrecked, until a Messerschmitt shot him down. He broke his first Spitfire by forgetting to lower his undercarriage before landing. His flight-commander – for they had just come back from ops – drew a revolver and put a bullet into his undercarriage so that the accident might be blamed upon enemy action. But a few flights later, he came in to land too low and crashed into the Spitfire of another squadron parked beside the perimeter track. Then no friend could save him and very ceremoniously he lost four months' seniority. As if that would matter!

Desmond Hughes trained along with me; he was an Irishman, with an Irishman's fertile imagination. When he spun a story about a shared adventure, it sounded so convincing, it left me goggle-eyed and wondering whether I had indeed been with him. Our RAF careers followed much the same pattern, yet he put in more operational flying than I, and survived the war, chalking up three times my score. Roger Barclay was a pleasant Cambridge undergraduate who confided in us that it had been his life's ambition to fly with the Air Force but that his parents had forbidden him to do so. The war gave him his chance; he made an excellent and studious pilot but was killed in the defence of Malta. Percy Burton from Johannesburg was the sixth; he was one of those who had tempted me into the university air squadron in the first place, now he was to be killed during the Battle of Britain, ramming an Me 110 and going down with it. Boost Fleming was the seventh of our number, a tough little chap, shot down in the Battle of Britain. The story, as I was told it, was that he crashed his Hurricane in flames, jumped out and ran around it. The other pilots, watching him from the air, laughed, thinking him safe and well but in fact he dropped dead. Pat Wells makes the eighth of our number. He was badly burned about the head during the day blitzes but recovered and with tettered face rejoined a squadron and survived the war. Hugh Percy, the owner of a giant green racing Bentley, made out reasonably until he was killed flying Spitfires during the Normandy landings. Roddy Knocker makes the tenth. He prospered until, after two serious crashes, his nerve failed and his doctors grounded him. I think there was another whose name and fate I have forgotten. This was now our little group, cheerfully ignorant of the future.

At Cranwell, we were both taught to fly and led gently into

the strange Air Force world. This world possessed not only an argot for the locker-room and the airman's mess but a technical jargon of some beauty, spoken in private cities as curiously named as Petra and Samarkand. Flying-boats from Calshot and Basra appeared in connection with navigation; with plumb-line distances and great circles, spot heights, verge and gimbal rings, lubber lines and directions like athwartships. These men led me by the hand into a world of hard-iron and soft-iron effects, of swinging the compass, of running fixes and graticules. The navigation officers, men otherwise with a full measure of human frailty, introduced us to the P4 compass and the P6 – what works of art they were! – to the tail drift sight and plumb-lines which should be hung upon the airscrew boss and tail skid. Navigators, permitted very properly to wear on their breasts only one wing, helped us to words such as aneroid barometer and Pitot tube and to such telling phrases as Admiralty Notices to Mariners. We were enriched.

Air Force cities, today as deserted as those venerable oases which the sands now cover, were then full of pride. Far up in the north, where winter is almost perpetual night, lay Sullom Voe and Sumburgh. There was Skeabrae in the Orkneys, alongside that race of water, Turnhouse at Edinburgh, Prestwick, Manorbier, Valley, Milford Haven, Portreath in the west, Exeter, Middle Wallop, Hullavington, Worthy Down, Tangmere, Manston in the south and to the east, Digby and Sutton Bridge, Martlesham Heath, North Weald. Place-names, to me now as remote as Maiden Castle!

With these, went terms associated with the overcast, governed by that inexact science, meteorology. At the feet of the lecturer upon this subject, we learnt about cirrus and altostratus, dew-points, synoptic weather charts, parallels of latitude, magnetic north, variation, equators and fields, cyclonic rain, the warm front and the Beaufort scale.

A lecturer who delighted us was a dry, humourless NCO, who informed us about the mechanism of a machine gun that at the humblest estimate was a war out-of-date. He neither joked nor smiled until one day he risked one droll story. Apparently, a year or so before this, a cadet had disobeyed orders and while low flying by the aerodrome, struck the telephone wires and crashed. 'Chopped his swede right off, it did,' he observed, 'but we could see the funny side of it.'

One instructor a few years before had been flying Vickers Wellesleys in Iraq. He described how occasional air-gunners returning from punitive operations against enemy villages, would take pot-shots at Arabs ploughing in the fields while they were low-flying home after the raid.

I myself made an indifferent pupil. The law of the conservation of energy is engrained in me. So when I had an instructor in the aeroplane, I used rather to let him fly it. He was, after all, much better at it than I was. This was not a success. But left to myself I learned fast. Indeed, I had to. For I was given but one night in which to learn night-flying. After an uncertain hour flying dual, I was sent solo in the early hours of a morning black as bitumen. The ambulance carried away my predecessor who had crashed his aircraft. As I walked uncertainly out to the Hind, past airmen squatting around a brazier like Africans, an unknown airman shouted to me out of the dark, 'Good luck.' I was most moved.

One evening, the rigger on my aircraft, of an age with the rest of us, and all smiles and blushes, begged me for my motorcar, saying that he would pay for the petrol. He was keen to go to a dance in Boston and to secure the car invited me to come too. For some preposterous reason I did not go. But a friend had discovered an old lady in a remote Derbyshire village who kept a single petrol pump. She had not heard of petrol rationing, so we drove off there each weekend to fill up. Her trade was so slight she could have come nearly through the war without coupons.

February had brought deep snow. Since flying was impossible, they emptied the college for a month. Then spring and early summer came, 1940. After four months of training, we were given our wings, and we were ready to leave Cranwell. It was the fashion in those days – perhaps the custom remains – for the outgoing course to put on a concert. Our concert was fun. The great evening came at last, the hall was filled and the show was on.

I cannot now remember too much of it. Uncle Filthy, an older pilot with a wooden leg, deep midnight shadow and a fund of foul stories, stumped onto the stage and told two of the dirtiest. One of them, if I remember aright, ended with him holding two potatoes in the air and exclaiming: 'And these are King Edwards.' David Scott-Malden, with gentle mimicry, took off Churchill and Roosevelt making their war speeches. 'They asked for guns, they shall have guns, etc, etc.' A pilot, suitably attired as a soprano, appeared at a casement window to sing a love-song which became, by easy stages, a rude parody of the military ditty 'Colonel Bogey'. One act, in which I was to have taken part until a highbrow heard me sing – upon which I was advised to put on tennis shoes and work the curtain – was a little marred by the absent-mindedness of Thomas Lund. Pat Dawley, our roly-poly Welsh tenor, appeared on the fore part of the stage, the proscenium, and struck up: 'Oooh! Who are the birdmen, the birdmen of England?' The curtain should then have lifted to display four birdmen dressed after the style of the bicyclists of Blériot's day, who broke into their own stirring version of the Yeomen of England. But when the curtain lifted it was only for three birdmen because Thomas Lund, true Thomas, had earlier wandered into the auditorium, so enjoying the show that he forgot he was himself due to take part. As soon as he recognised that he was absent, however, he hastened to the back and being incorrectly attired, intoned his entire solo from behind the scenery.

Someone who saw Holmes in the audience, a pilot of the previous war and our senior instructor, reported that the tears were running down his cheeks. He was, perhaps, too keenly aware of the deaths impending for most of the actors.

# Chapter 4

# Advanced Training

I was at this time surprised to discover how readily friends would change their characters to suit different circumstances. Thus a soldier, on being commissioned, changes; from being Sergeant Smith he becomes Lieutenant Smith. He believes that Lieutenant Smith requires a different sort of character from Sergeant Smith and so he alters himself. As he is promoted, he changes again; for Major Smith must be a different sort of man from Captain Smith and Captain Smith from Lieutenant Smith. By the hour he has become Colonel Smith his own character has often disappeared, so that he becomes in fact merely 'the Colonel'. Watching a specific personality in this way hardening and dying enthralled me.

Another kindred and surprising development for me lay in the acceptance of situation. 'My dear, I have forty-eight hours and then I must return to France.' The pathos of it! He had seen war films, he had read war books; and so, as he walked down Piccadilly, he made that sort of comment.

For my part, I decided that I would not budge an inch; that, whatever happened, I should remain a sort of undergraduate and amateur naturalist; and that out of self-respect, I should always speak frankly and say just what I thought. This rather unmilitary and uncivil resolve led me to some lively quarrels. Inevitably, of course, and without noticing it, I budged a great deal.

For I began, much against my wish, to find myself quite at

home in the Air Force. I came to this by stages, since it was another two years before I could accept this galling truth. At this time I began to feel easier. I was now flying alone, and being no longer cursed with information, rapidly settled and grew to feel secure in the narrow cockpit, resting on precarious wings. Flight has always remained something of a miracle to me; and the life aloft required a perpetual act of faith, a materialist's *credo quia absurdum.*

For it is a strange experience. Anyone who has learned to fly will remember the cumbersome flying suit in which he was swaddled, the helmet, the ear-phones, the mask, the gloves. Then he is strapped around with a parachute harness, which tangles with the Gosford speaking-tubes, and over the parachute harness go the safety straps, which lash him to the seat. The whole truss is inconceivably uncomfortable until he becomes inured to it, and is designed to lower a pupil's mental and physical efficiency to the lowest possible point. It makes him a bird with wet wings. I remember such a time when my respect for the brothers Orville and Wilbur Wright altogether disappeared. It was a cold day in March. We were to do slow rolls, Flying Officer Chater informed me. It was really quite easy. You choose a fixed point on the empty horizon and roll around it. Get your speed up to 150 mph, raise the nose above the horizon to that point; apply a little rudder with stick hard over, over you go; opposite rudder to stop the yaw; stick well forward to keep the nose up while you are inverted; a little more rudder to help you over and there you are. It is as simple as that.

The weather was clear. The countryside below was divided neatly into its mosaic of woods and green fields, a lake, a park, the cold beauty of the early year. 'I will show you a slow roll,' said Chater, and over we went. The biplane hung upside down. The Kestrel engine spluttered and cut. There was a strange quietness except for the soughing of the wind in the flying-wires. 'It is quite easy,' a voice said, and then wrathfully, 'don't hang on to the stick.' For, as any pilot knows, there is give in the harness that ties you to the seat, and if it is in addition none too tightly fastened, you dangle horribly in the air half in and out of the cockpit. We glided upside down. As I looked at the pretty world above, as timid as I have ever been in an aeroplane, I murmured lugubriously: 'What one does for King and Country!'

We practised for a while. A voice asked: 'Have you ever done an inverted spin?' 'No!' 'Wouldn't you care to do one?' 'No!' 'I am sure you would,' he coaxed. 'I am sure I wouldn't,' I replied. 'I am sure you would. I will show you what they are like. They are easier to come out of than an ordinary spin.' And so Chater attempted it. The forces at work during an inverted spin press you out from the cockpit. You not only hang upside down, but, as the aircraft flicks around, you are hurled outwards; the blood rushes to the head and the eyes are pulled from their fastenings in the socket. Fortunately, Chater's nerve failed. We walked about the sky upside down while he kicked at the rudder but we never completed that manoeuvre.

This tutelage was soon over. For, shortly afterwards we were sent to Sealand, near Liverpool, to fly our first aircraft with retractable undercarriages. They were Masters, an advanced trainer which possessed the characteristics of the contemporary fighter. We were thrilled by them. I remember to this day how gladly I flew along the estuary of the Ribble, and along the sunlit coasts of North Wales. We chased each other in mock dog-fights. We were persuaded we should join fighter squadrons, until, after two or three days, they posted us to Old Sarum, the school for Army Co-operation pilots.

Old Sarum was the small, hump-backed, undulating aerodrome near Salisbury. It then boasted two types of aircraft: Hectors, which were biplanes, all very slow and very old-fashioned; and Lysanders, which the simple generals supposed to be the latest thing for Army flying. You sat upright in the Lysander cockpit, much like a London taxi-driver, with your feet turned out on the pedals. A gunner with a single, gas-operated Vickers machine-gun worked it manually from the seat behind.

I did not fancy this. The course of pupils that left the school before we arrived, largely died, if I remember aright, dropping supplies to the Guards regiment at Calais, two days after the last man of it had surrendered.

They set us to take photographs. We made line overlaps in case anyone wished to make a map. We pinpointed ponds in fields and photographed village churches. We were becoming quite adept in these old-fashioned, and, to our way of thinking, ill-conceived aircraft, until after a week or so the order came through that we were to be sent to Aston Down, an advanced fighter training station in Gloucestershire. I was naturally as exhilarated as all the others to leave a job for which I had no stomach. With the fall of Dunkirk, there was no army with which to co-operate, so we were to train as fighter-pilots for the next stage of the war, the threatening invasion. We had finally realised the height of our ambitions. The weather was fine. My eyes and nose were running with hay-fever.

The teaching staff at Aston Down was largely drawn from the pilots of No 1 Squadron, the Hurricane squadron that had acquitted itself so well in France under the leather-jacketed 'Bull' Halahan. Halahan was now in charge of our fighter training and what he said, went. By God! Pat Dawley remained in Army Co-operation; the remaining eleven of us were divided up; seven to train on Spitfires; four to train on Defiants; these last were Roddy Knocker, Hugh Percy, Desmond Hughes and myself. We began by flying Fairey Battles, a gentle aircraft, one that was too slow and ill-armed for the unescorted missions on which it was first despatched. The squadrons of camouflaged Battles, light undersides, dun and green above, which I had seen drawn up in line on Abingdon aerodrome ready to leave for France in 1939, were by now utterly destroyed; frequently, it seemed to me, because they had been faultily used. The burly Halahan, when he appointed the four of us to fly Defiants, described Defiants, I remember his words, as 'the answer to the maiden's prayer'. However, no instructor at Aston Down had any experience of proper Defiant tactics, so after ten days or so we were sent off to join our fighter squadron. It was then the middle of June.

There were two tricks which the pupil at Aston Down designed to try before he left. Like many another pupil I was sufficiently green and foolish to attempt them both. The aerodrome was laid out across high ground. There was a deep, narrow valley beside it in which lies the town of Stroud. The first trick was to fly down the valley and slow-roll below the level of the surrounding ground; this was not too difficult and you could cheat a little. Hugh Percy led me into the next, while I was flying formation on him. He was leading and we were flying low down the River Severn in our Defiants. As we approached the bridge I expected him to lift over it. Not a bit of it, he headed for one span and I, accepting the challenge, took its neighbour. I muttered a prayer, aimed for the centre of the span, and through we roared. This circus act became less popular at a later date, for someone crashed when taking a Blenheim through.

When I could, I used to visit Alan Howe at his gamekeeper's cottage. I would break off a training flight to dive low over his house; while he or his children waved at me towels, table-cloths or anything white in return. It was a frequent and pleasant greeting.

So our brief training ended. The four of us, the Defiant pilots, were posted to 264 Squadron, the City of Madras Squadron, then stationed at Duxford aerodrome, near Cambridge. We were now entering the maelstrom, and in a curious way I think we were looking foward to it all.


## THE DREAM

The young pilot in full flying-kit slept.

He dreamt he was a white lambkin with the double wings of a butterfly — yet vaguely the lamb resembled the swinging sign of the Admiral Benbow – and he zoomed upwards and upwards so that the clouds beneath him were akin to a layer of white tiles on the bathroom floor at home.

There was a blue sky above. Yet was he not inside the dome of St Pauls? There, in his niche stood St Albert Ball, there St Billy Bishop, there St Augustine Trenchard, there St Richthofen and, with his face averted, there one of the lesser Armenian saints, St Immelman, celebrated for his turn.

Now it was sky again. A great winged dragon appeared from nowhere—Jabberwocky—and with talons outstretched and with visible scales, sought to turn upon and destroy the lamb; the lamb which breathed blood or fire and with incredible courage, fantastically outnumbered, buried its teeth in the jugular vein of the dragon, snap, snap, snap.

As the anaconda lay dying, a voice like a chinagraph pencil was heard to praise: 'Well done, thou good and faithful servant.' And an old and whiskered man, like the pilot's father, rose and pinned into his snow-white fleece a medal, which was a course and track computer.

The lamb, tears of self-congratulation rolling from his eyes, folded his wings into a small suitcase and then lay dying from his too-great exertion.

I served my country faithfully, he bleated, before all went dark.

# Chapter 5

# 264 Squadron: Waiting for the Invasion

'He was a fine gentleman, Sir. And this one, Sir, I never looked after a better officer.' Our arrival at Duxford was cinema. Two nights before, a small force of German bombers, in day camouflage, their bellies still sprayed white, had flown in over East Anglia; 19 Squadron, who shared Duxford aerodrome with us, had engaged them. The old batman, a peace-time servant, was giving us the bedrooms of the few casualties; their family photographs and their soiled clothes, smelling of sweat, were still scattered around. Hugh Percy lit upon one of their log-books. Its owner must have been a conceited fellow, we thought, for he had entered such comments about himself as – 'Gave a much-admired display of aerobatics.' 'Did beautiful rolls.'

We then reported to the squadron adjutant, Kimber, and approved of him. He regretted, he said, that he could not go out with us that evening as he was engaged. A voice asked, 'Who to?' The elderly adjutant paused a second before replying – 'To whom!'

I was introduced to my gunner, Scott. He was a young, green and very nice New Zealander, small, innocent, healthy. If I suggested anything he said, 'Good O, Sir.'

Then followed for us lazy, sunlit days in Cambridgeshire, lying on the sward beside our fighters, waiting for the invasion. We were given little or no ammunition with which our gunners might train because most of it had been left behind in France. Instead, we dropped practice bombs on imaginary landing-barges and laid smoke, smoke which would have become, had the invasion started, mustard gas. Just after daybreak, German aircraft used to sneak in, using cloud. We chased them often, but I do not recollect that any of us ever saw one. We practised formation flying, and studied toy models of German bombers, their gun positions and their fields of fire.

I came to know more about my strange profession. Our fellow pilots were mostly members of the peace-time air force, many holding short-service commissions. As such, they were men with a quite different outlook from the wandering scholars; but we settled in, and grew, I allow, rather more to be like them than they like us. They used to rib me personally upon the fact that I did not need to shave every morning. I replied that people grew most hair on the parts that they used most and this kept the half-bald gentlemen with their handlebar moustaches quieter.

Our Squadron-Commander, Philip Hunter, enjoyed prestige and our confidence. He had led the squadron with conspicuous success during the period when it covered the army's final retreat to Dunkirk and the subsequent evacuation. The other pilots drew a picture of the dense clouds of smoke they encountered over the harbour and the confused air-fighting inland of it. We four students were replacements for the casualties that were then sustained. When we arrived, the squadron score stood at sixty-four; and it had established a record of thirty-seven German aircraft destroyed in one day, without loss to itself. I no longer believe these figures, since I later discovered how easy it was for gunners each to claim a plane that was actually shared. Nevertheless, Philip Hunter's results were most impressive, and morale was as high as it should be.

At this time 19 Squadron occupied 'G1', the reserve landing ground just a few fields away from us. Of a summer's evening they used to practise rocket loops, diving low over their airfield, climbing straight into the quiet azure, thence toppling over backward to begin their dive once more. They were flies above a summer river before the rise.

I was always jealous of these Spitfire pilots for possessing an aircraft more fluent than my own, a single-seater, the last word in nimbleness and power. I think that it was Spitfires from the aerodrome of Digby that persuaded me, when they took off, a section rising into the air like a spring of teal. For in the last light of a warm day one of their pilots used to fly up the Roman road, Ermine Street, which runs past Cranwell, and in the dove-blue of the evening leisurely roll. Then, one afternoon, when the air was burdened with big, white cumulus, with shafts of light splitting the cathedral gloom, a Spitfire dived across the front of me, coming out of one chasm in the trailing cloud, diving to where I could see Digby fighter-station camouflaged below. It was entrancing.

Group-Captain Woodhall, our most popular Station-Commander, lectured us on fighting right across England if it should ever become necessary. Our first backward step, if our part of East Anglia were captured, would be to the airfield at the Caxton Gibbet. Fortunately, it was never needed.

Somewhere around this time I had the pleasure of seeing behind the station adjutant's desk, in response to a threat issued by Croft in the Lords, a pike. It was a broom-handle tipped with a point of iron, with which, according to station orders, he would doubtless have repulsed the invading Hun.

We slept in a Nissen hut next to our aircraft. When I went to bed, I slept, enjoying the deep animal sleep of youth. I died each night and was reluctantly resurrected in the morning. But that now ended. For I was woken one night by someone shouting. It was 3.45 and beginning to be light. I turned over and tried to slumber, yet even as I closed my eyes, it came to me that all the others were strangely active. Someone was shouting, 'Hell and beggary, where are my trousers?' So I woke again, to see in the twilight the last of my fellows strapping on his Mae West and stumbling out. It was my first alarm. I forced myself out of bed, the air blew cold and it smelt freshly of hay.

My clothes were in disorder; so I slipped coat and trousers

over my pyjamas. I jumped into flying-boots, grabbed my Mae West and ran through the darkness for the shadow of the aircraft. Being the most junior pilot, my aircraft was the slowest in the squadron and the furthest off. I thought afterwards that it would have been a more sensible arrangement if matters had been the other way round. When I reached my old Defiant, I tried to be sick. I wasn't sick however, so I clambered onto the metal wing and dropped into the cockpit, where my parachute awaited me. Scott slipped into the turret behind.

The engine started. As the prop turned, it blew the dew off the rounded, perspex windscreen. I skimped warming the engine, and taxied out in time, note it, to join the second section.

I could not find the knob for the variable-pitch propeller. My section leader began to roll forward across the sappy green turf of Duxford. I opened up, we roared over the ground in the chilly twilight of a Cambridgeshire dawn. I had full throttle, but Yellow 1 and Yellow 2 pulled away from me. It was obviously an emergency, so I used the emergency handle which gave the engine extra power. Even then, I only just cleared the far hedge. Something was wrong, for the engine was only giving 1500 revs. I searched the cockpit. I found that on the previous day they had changed the propeller on this aircraft from a variable-pitch to a constant-speed air-screw and I had taken off in full course.

I put matters to rights and joined up with John Banham, my section leader. I was cold and excited, indeed I had never been able to fly a decent formation anyway. Then my knees started to knock. Until that moment I had heard of the expression but I had always believed it to be figurative, not descriptive. They banged each other inside the pyjamas. I could mock their antics in a detached sort of way but I could in no wise control them.

I saw 'B' Flight taking off far beneath us and joining up in formation below us. They climbed up towards us. The white bellies of the three Defiants ahead of me resembled the firm white flesh of fish. It was growing properly light. I had always been pretty sceptical about the invasion, now I wondered if landings had actually occurred. In a tight formation of twelve Defiants we paraded East Anglia: Cambridge, Thetford, Yarmouth, Southwold, Orford Ness and back, proud of our strength. It was a summer morning and the season for haymaking. In some meadows the grass still rippled sensuously as the wind stirred it, in some the hay was cut, and it lay in ripe swathes waiting for the dew on it to dry. The ranks of wheat were yellowing.

There had been no other aircraft in the sky; yet Storrs, one of our gunners, swore that as we flew over Norfolk a man, without a parachute, dropped past his turret. He refused to be talked out of it. I, Münchhausenwise, wondered if perhaps an airman from the previous war had been caught up in an eddy, and had travelled Europe ever since, too high and too cold to disintegrate. When we returned to base, we were told that we had been called out on a false alarm.

# Chapter 6

# A Greenhorn's Battle of Britain

Attacks on convoys increased. We started to fly forward at dawn to Martlesham Heath, to help protect the convoys that were off the low-lying coasts of Suffolk and Essex. Then the Battle of Britain warmed up in earnest. We were next sent to Kirton-in-Lindsay, an airfield in Lincolnshire. But before we left, the first Czech fighter squadron arrived on Duxford aerodrome. So our officers threw a sherry party for them. Talking mostly in French and German they were cheerful about the R A F aircraft, maintaining that we equipped them to a more workmanlike style than had the French. Some days later the Station-Commander received a letter from an irate mother in the district, complaining that a Czech airman had bitten off one of her daughter's tits.

We awaited the invasion, not greatly perturbed. No one that I knew expected defeat, although propaganda is seductive for a young mind. I did not myself have enough history to be able to put this historic battle into perspective; instead, I was aware that the German Army and the German Air Force were much more numerous than our own. I knew that they commanded the resources of all Europe and were backed by a Treaty of Friendship with Soviet Russia. Churchill had broadcast that if necessary we should fight from Canada. The grey-clad Wehrmacht had rolled across Europe even as it pleased. It would be hard then to explain to someone, only concerned in the war after the Germans had been measured up to, how truly frightening it is to be a youngster pitted against a measureless enemy, with his rumoured exhibitions of vast military might, an unknown Leviathan, an armoured Behemoth. I had listened on the radio to some of Hitler's principal speeches punctuated by thunderous and menacing applause, with their dominating Heil!! Heil!! Heil!! I believe that Housman, in his verse written on the Mercenaries best explains what my more skilled contemporaries achieved:

Their shoulders held the sky suspended,
They stood, and Earth's foundations stay.

It became a study of mine, one I pursued meticulously at this time, to discover what type of man makes the best fighter-pilot. I found, for example, that only children, pilots without brothers or sisters, were particularly helpless. When a new pilot came to us, I would try to guess after a day or two whether he came from a large family or not and then go and ask him. If he did, he had a better chance to survive. Good pilots are common, good fighter-pilots were rare. It is as with polo: many can ride, but few play polo well; and among those who play well, many ride in a crude and efficient way, without good hands or precision. I arrived at few conclusions. The qualities that made for success in a fighter-pilot seemed to be just those sturdy qualities that made for success in other professions; observation, initiative, determination, courage, including the courage to run away. In course of time it appeared that men who had a private axe to grind beyond the public axe of the King's enemies were especially successful. In a secular sense it is indeed true to say that 'The Lord gets his best soldiers out of the highlands of affliction.' Stevens, who was perhaps the most remarkable night-fighter-pilot of the war, had lost his wife and children in the bombing of Hull. He was therefore only interested in killing more and more Germans in revenge. Guy Gibson, at one time with us as a chubby night-fighter-pilot, went for medals and fame; achieving both in Bomber Command before he was eventually killed. Bob Braham, another outstanding pilot in our profession, had grown into the way of killing, seemingly almost for the sake of it. He proved most adept until eventually taken prisoner in Denmark when the Germans gave a special dinner for him before locking him away.

On July 19th, the squadron took off to reinforce London but were turned back. They then received orders, later counter-manded, to fly to Edinburgh the next day.

In the middle of August, after the day-fighting had been maintained for some time, we flew to Hornchurch, the main sector station east of London and north of the river. Its two satellite landing-grounds and advanced airfields were on the coast, Manston and Rochford, near Southend. This was talked about as 'hell-fire corner'. We were ordered to go forward to Rochford next day. While Philip Hunter, our Commanding Officer, was drinking coffee after dinner out of the small mess coffee cups, we began to chat informally and I suggested to him that it was quite wrong that a Defiant squadron should be the first off against the enemy, as we would be expected to be the next morning. The Defiant was slow, had a low rate-of-climb, was a little helpless against enemy fighters but was a magnificent destroyer of bombers. We should be the last, not the first squadron, I argued. Philip Hunter did not deny the facts but he said that we were in the place of honour and must accept it. I think that by this means we threw away the advantage of our peculiar aircraft, and from this our misfortunes stemmed.

I was too green to be permitted to fly the next day. The squadron, however, was caught by German fighters as it took off from Rochford and Philip Hunter was among those who were trapped against the sea and killed. This was a double disaster, for we lost our good Squadron-Commander and they appointed in his place a man without the requisite experience or character.

It was my fortune in those days, being among the youngest,

to wait long hours at readiness, and then when a 'flap' did occur, a more senior pilot would rush down, fiddle my aeroplane from me and leave me behind, cursing him. After one or two actions when we encountered mixed success, ardour waned; so that I and my new and able gunner, John Hardie, could take the air. Flight-Lieutenant Ash, the senior gunner, had removed from me my excellent New Zealander. Hardie, however, was one of the ablest gunners in the squadron, an Englishman grown up in India, a cool, solid sort of sergeant with whom I was privileged to be crewed.

The squadron went forward again to Rochford, where we refuelled and awaited advice to take off. I was nicely placed, being Yellow 2, or on the right-hand side of the second section. We were flying in sections of three aircraft, in V formation, the sections being in line astern – a handy squadron formation for our type of aircraft. 'Bull' Whitley, a chunk of marbled English beef was my section leader; a good fellow who had already gone out of his way to befriend me. Our Flight-Commander, John Banham, had been shot down into the sea two days before and was left behind to dry out.

It was the practice to announce over the aerodrome loud-speakers how the enemy attack was developing. Radar permitted us to watch as it built up over France; squadrons would be alerted, and a running commentary broadcast by the Station-Commander of German behaviour and then the subsequent battle. The phrase used was 'They're boiling up', and one pictured Luftwaffe squadrons forming up over Cherbourg into wing and group formations for a surprise attack that was rarely, in fact, a surprise.

A formation of Dorniers had bombed Hornchurch two days before. Being left on the ground as usual, I had been able to follow the fighting from the Tannoy system. Then I watched the formation of Dorniers, tiny specks, glinting lethally in the sunlight, approach us on its bombing run, where we were the target. As the formation drew overhead, we crowded into the bomb-bays. Derrick Smythe, Hugh Percy's humorous South African gunner, found a cart-horse abandoned by its driver and struggled to wedge it into the air-raid shelter after us. The long stick of bombs began to burst, running up towards us. A voice cried: 'Lie down.' Panic scythed the crowd and all lay as one man. The explosions stopped short of us. The stick killed six civilians and three cows.

But soon it was my turn to fight. I had over two hundred hours' flying and a great deal more confidence in my ability than my ability warranted. It is more than twenty years since that day and the first details now escape me. But I remember that we crossed the Thames and the Medway, leaving the towns with their moorings of toy balloons far beneath. But we were not climbing fast enough. Our new Squadron-Commander could not lock up the wheels of his Defiant. I can see them now, flopping out of their housing, to be hydraulically raised again. He was wasting time. There they were! There they were!

A flock of Heinkels were coming in past Folkestone, making towards London. White puffs of smoke followed them. We were at seventeen thousand feet, three-and-a-half-miles up; but far above us, still small black motes in the empyrean, the top cover of Messerschmitts drove in. I concentrated on keeping my place in the formation, for I was a bad formation-flier, but as I glanced up again I saw that our own fighters were attacking the top cover. The plan was excellent but we ourselves were too low, too low. Then it happened.

I was on the right side of our formation, my left, gauntleted hand upon the throttle, the cockpit hood back a space to allow an uninterrupted view. A fighter – ours or theirs I did not see – a casualty from the fight above, dropped past me, quite close, in perpendicular dive for the ground. I watched him, fascinated, peering over the side to keep my eye on him. He never paused, never halted, but accelerated and accelerated for the deck. Perhaps the pilot was dead over the controls; or perhaps alive, his controls and his hood jammed, he was unable to escape. A crimson light flashed through a green Kentish wood almost before he hit.

We described a half circle under the formation of Heinkels and then proceeded to climb up under them and a little to one flank. I noticed that we had only 160 mph on the clock. They were about twenty or thirty large Heinkels flying in sections of three, line astern. My gunner began to fire. I concentrated on keeping formation, confident that the whole of 'B' Flight was behind, protecting my tail. The four Brownings stuttered above my head. I became excited. 'Bull' Whitley moved over and sat just in front of me. Both Bill Carnaby and ourselves pulled Heinkels out of the formation. Ours – I never saw it – fell out with flames pouring from one engine, or so Hardie told me later. Then Hardie started to fire at a second. The Heinkels looked as big as elephants.

I had felt jolts or rattles on my own aircraft, however, and a voice seemed to say down the intercom: 'I'm wounded.' I flicked over, pulled back on the stick, and spiralled for the ground in a controlled blackout. At ground level I straightened out.

'Are you all right?' I shouted to the air-gunner down our faulty radio.

'Quite all right.'

'I thought you said you were wounded?'

'No!' he said. 'Turn to starboard.'

Then the engine died, although we had petrol, oil pressure and correct temperatures. I moved the throttle but there was no response. The switches were on. We were two hundred feet up over Kent. I looked for a convenient field, finding them all, however, studded with poles to forestall German gliders.

It had been a warm August, the Kentish clay was dry and caked. I had earlier resolved that if I had to make an emergency landing, I would for comfort cushion it into the brush top of a hedge. Just such a hedge was handy, so we dodged between the poles, crashed through the brush and landed comfortably on the verge at the other side. Gunners had earned the reputation in our squadron of being out of the turret of a crashed aircraft before it had actually crashed. Hardie was no exception. He was peering into my cockpit before I had raised a cut nose from the instrument panel into which it had banged.

'Are you okay?'

'All right,' I said.

'You only just slipped under the high-tension cables.'

'What cables?' I turned round and saw them for the first time. I had noticed some odd poles among the rest as I came in, but had been too busy to observe what they carried.

Then we heard a blue note and the rattle of machine-guns. A Messerschmitt 109 was diving for the ground with a Hurricane hard upon its tail, pumping lead into him. The pilot parachuted in the nick of time, his aircraft plunging into the earth three fields away.

'Won't you come in and have a drink?' asked the vicar, stepping out of the vicarage of Petham, in front of which we had all so dramatically and irreligiously landed.

'Thank you,' I replied. Prior to joining him, I looked over the aircraft in an attempt to discover the cause of failure. A cannon shell had exploded in the turret, jamming two of the guns. The ammunition chutes had taken the blast, thus saving Hardie. The fuselage itself was well peppered, the underside of it could not be examined.

The vicar pressed his whisky on us. I had only once before drunk whisky. The infantry sent a truck over to take us back to their mess. They pressed whisky on us again. They thought that our nerves had been affected. I think we were jubilant, however. We reckoned we had bagged a Heinkel in our first fight – they could probably patch up our machine – and most important, we had made all the standard boobs and survived them. Hardie explained that when he said: 'Turn to starboard' there were four Messerschmitts behind us. 'B' Flight, he said, had been shot down or gone home long ago, and we were acting as 'Arse-end-Charlie'.

In the mess, elegant young army officers complained to me that the RAF monopolised the war; anyway, they lisped, we ourselves have nothing to shoot with. For their guns had all been abandoned in France. The Messerschmitt pilot was locked up in a horse-box, which led me to point out the advantage of fighting over one's own country. I then went to interview the German. He was pale and shaken, and he complained of a sore back, so I obtained a mattress for him to lie upon. He claimed to have shot down a Defiant that morning. He said that, in general, he judged Spitfires to be better than Messerschmitts, Hurricanes not so good, and Defiants no good at all. This summary grieved me. He was too sore and suspicious to talk much. But he alarmed me by his appearance, for in place of the muscle-knotted Siegfried I had come to expect of the Nazis, he seemed to be the typical jeweller from the Old Kent Road. Had I seen him first, I thought, I should never have allowed a middle-aged character like that to shoot me down.

We had been reported missing until our telephone messages reached base. We returned by train. Fitted out in flying-suits, fur-boots, parachutes, helmets, etc, we were knights without horses. Anyway, it was a romantic way of crossing London.

Returning to the aerodrome, we heard the worst of the news. 'Bull' Whitley and his gunner had been killed, leaving me with the feeling that had I been much more wide-awake I could have saved my friend and supporter. Shaw, who had been flying in the aircraft behind me, was dead; someone else was in hospital, the Squadron-Commander's plane had caught fire; he and his expert gunner, Flight-Lieutenant Ash, had jumped for it, but his gunner was found to be dead on reaching the ground with three bullets in him. For the following sortie that afternoon, there were only two aircraft fit to take the air. We were hushed all the next day, quietly subdued in the mess.

They ordered us back to Kirton-in-Lindsay. Our morale remained excellent. We were all convinced that given proper leadership, we would do as well over London as the squadron had previously done during the hectic week over Belgium and Holland. I think that our squadron scored in that week of fighting around London, nineteen German aircraft destroyed, with six other German aircraft damaged or probably destroyed.

# Chapter 7

# The Night Attacks:
# Kirton-in-Lindsay and
# Gravesend

Then came the night of the invasion scare, September 8th, when the church bells rang around us. I was woken at midnight by Fellowes, our Intelligence Officer, who said the news had come through that the expected invasion had started. I pretended to be unconcerned, but yet I was tense and overwrought. We were soon up for an early dawn patrol, but nothing came of it. London was very heavily bombed throughout the night.

After my mishap over Kent, I had formed several resolutions. I determined: never to trust anyone except myself; not to be bound by orders but to make my own decisions; never to be frightened again. I relapsed from this at times, but not, I think, for too long. Our squadron had been originally earmarked for night-fighting. We now began night-training in earnest; and from September onwards, the day alerts became increasingly a side-line.

It was apparent that the Royal Air Force had begun the war with a night-bomber policy but without a night-fighter policy. In peace-time, private pilots had been paid to fly at night to give the defences practice, for, so it was said, Fighter Command broke so many aircraft when they flew in the dark it was uneconomical to continue with it. Fighter Command began the war with three or four squadrons of Blenheim fighters, carrying a primitive form of radar; but as frequently the fighter was slower than the bomber it was chasing, they were none too successful. From the ground there was little assistance. Our radios, sets called TR9, were unreliable and inadequate. Occasionally they were tuned to the same wave-length as the German aircraft we were chasing, with amusing results. On one occasion we heard a German pilot singing 'September in the Rain'. The searchlights were commanded by gallant officers of artillery or cavalry from the previous war, who knew little or nothing about aircraft. We depended upon them, and upon the Observer Corps for their guidance from the ground. Assuredly the latter tried; but as they relied on their ears – and many gaffers, we suspected, were a trifle deaf – none of us profited much.

It became apparent during the day-fighting that a small nucleus of pilots held a squadron together. Out of a squadron, perhaps four or five old hands could be trusted to go up and come back again each sortie, every now and then with another swastika for the side of their machines. New pilots came and died, the veterans stayed. They would land on the advanced airfield, roll and bump their hunch-backed planes to the hedge and begin a game of poker until it was time to take off.

A night-fighter squadron came even more to depend upon its veterans. For the newer pilots could not be led into a fight; each man travelled through the dark alone. Our craft became increasingly technical. We later held that it took a new pilot, after a much longer period of training than we enjoyed, a full year on an operational squadron before he knew his work and could be trusted to fly in any weather. At this stage, however, we were all unpractised and all without proper equipment.

During September the Germans switched over from day to night attacks, attacks which became ever more heavy as the year declined. We were supposed to protect Hull and the Humber, the manufacturing cities of the Midlands and the bomber aerodromes ranged along the East Coast. We improved, and our equipment improved, and as we improved we began to fly in thicker weather. That winter, I seemed to watch from the air most cities in England flame, but there was as yet little any of us could do about it.

The Order of Battle of our own bombing aircraft, this winter, saw what heavy aircraft the RAF possessed, massed along the East Coast. They stamped their personalities upon the country-side. The largest and slowest of them were the Whitleys, chiefly based in Yorkshire, at Pocklington, Driffield, Topcliffe, York, Linton-upon-Ouse. When I flew over their bases by day, they reposed ominously within their bomb-bays or in front of blocky, camouflaged hangers, so many carnivores sleeping until the dark.

The Handley-Page bombers, the Hampdens, were based in Lincolnshire and Nottinghamshire, with their twin rudders and unnaturally slender fuselages; these were at Hemswell, Wadding-ton, Scampton, Coleby Grange and Cottesmore; the crews being trained at Upper Heyford. This is as I remember it.

Further south, Wellingtons were based in Norfolk and Cam-bridgeshire, at Bassingbourn, Wyton, Bourn, Steeple Morden. They had fat, geodetic frames and were the most efficient of these early bombers.

The Fairey Battles that had not been destroyed in France had been finished off bombing the landing-barges that were mustered in the invasion ports. But Blenheims, a light, twin-engined craft with a glass nose, operated from the coastal aerodromes of East Anglia, their crews being trained at Bicester.

These were the vessels which were supposed to set fire to the cities of Germany. And indeed, not Germany alone, for all Europe was forcibly combined against us. The crews were too few, so that they died or were taken prisoner almost to a man. To this day I can see aircraft straining from the ground in the last, sad light of an exhausted evening and hear them throb visibly overhead. *Requiescant in pace*! – both the crews who died and those people whom they themselves destroyed in the cities of Germany. Bitter nights, light ebbing from and failing above the stubble and potato fields of Lincolnshire; frost and the flicker of stars. Before dawn the valley mist would roll over the fields and muffle all. Woe betide the crews who had not returned from the Ruhr before North Sea stratus and river mist had joined together in one blanket from the English sea-coast to the Pennines.

About this time we received a small sunburnt gunner, who had a wooden leg and a long history. His proper name was Sid Carlin, but he was known to us all as 'Timbertoes'. If I remember rightly he was an infantryman in 1914. He lost a leg, however, so he applied to join the Royal Flying Corps who would not accept him. He therefore taught himself to fly at his own expense, joining the RFC as a pilot. He rose to be the Commanding Officer of Billy Bishop's old squadron, 85 Squadron, but was shot down and taken prisoner. He was caught in the wire, he argued, only because of his wooden leg. Anyhow, he passed the inter-war years sailing an Arab dhow along the east coast of Africa. With the resumption of the war, he joined up again; and here he was with us in that noble and dangerous position of a junior Air Gunner. His DFC, we were amused to notice, began his second row of medals. He was continuously critical of the pre-war government in Britain, roundly denouncing it, particularly for lack of an agricultural policy. This was his hobby-horse. About this time we spent an evening in the Officers' Club at Grimsby, where a few local popsies were present. By midnight, all, save Timbertoes, had flagged. As he hobbled past one of us he whispered: 'I'm dancing with my first white woman for eighteen years.' Later he was killed when the Germans strafed the aerodrome from which he was operating, and in place of ducking, he attempted to shoot back from the turret of a parked aircraft.

Our practice at this time was to leave Lincolnshire in the afternoon for Ringway Aerodrome, near Manchester; re-fuel there and patrol the sea-approaches to Liverpool until dark. Then we flew, most nights, over the hills back to Lincolnshire, and were available to fly again from there. I sometimes felt that we resembled Beau Geste, who ran from embrasure to embrasure firing his rifle, in order to persuade the Arabs that the Foreign Legion remained on its feet. While sleeping at Ringway, one night, I was woken by five bombs aimed at the flare-path, which missed us all.

About this time, a request was sent round for training night-fighter pilots to re-form 85 Squadron. Our Commanding Officer had stolen my air-gunner, Hardie, from me. I was anxious to fly Hurricanes, single-seater fighters, where this sort of change could not happen. For the relation of pilot and gunner was close and conjugal. Bill Carnaby, a tall, suave auxiliary also volunteered, and our most cheerful Flight-Commander. Our Flight-Commander was refused, Bill and I went.

Upon arrival at our destination we felt sad. Why, we asked, had we deserted our friends? We decided that the three of us had consumed too good a lunch that day we volunteered. If only we had not drunk so much!

Our new unit was commanded by the finest Squadron-Commander I ever served under. I had met Peter Townsend at Martlesham Heath, when he had just been fished out of the sea. It was something like that, anyway. Also, someone had blown off a toe; so that he hobbled around with a stick, looking every inch the wounded hero. He had a dry, sarcastic manner which protected a sensitive man from being hurt. His adjutant, Tim Moloney, was a bookmaker by trade, a generous, well-given bachelor, very much an uncle to all his pilots. The rest of the squadron were of many nations; many of them being survivors of the fighting over France as well as over Britain. My nine months with these people were the toughest and most exhausting of my career. I shot nothing but I was taught my trade by them.

In two or three days, 264 Squadron went south and 85 Squadron flew from Church Fenton back to Kirton-in-Lindsay. There we trained, patrolled and hoped for something to turn up. I think now that one of the happiest features of the RAF was the chance acquaintances. Pilots tended to be the most adventurous of the young. In the first years of the war they were handpicked. It was above all an international force; and you might come across in the mess, although many were dull and disagreeable enough, many pleasant youngsters from all parts of the world. Their squadron, perhaps, was stationed with us a day, then it passed on. I learnt an international chess; today a Norwegian attack, next week a Polish defence.

Just such a chance acquaintance was a twenty-year-old Spitfire pilot nicknamed 'Junior'. I never knew his real name. 'Everyone calls me "Junior", you know.' He was a very humorous young-ster and I spent an uproarious evening with him in the bar. Next day, he caught a packet over France.

Another acquaintance was a Scot, Sinclair. He used to go round London calling himself General Sikorski's nephew, for its effect on the girls. I went to a Kent pub with him one night. The barman started: 'My boy Sid got seven days CB, he did, for not bathing. Said 'e'd seen enough water at Dunkirk. Funny thing, some time back a Spitfire came down by the Medway here, burning he was. Pilot had broken right away from his harness, fell quite slowly, funny thing, wasn't it, funny thing.' Two yokels came to us: 'Don't often get a chance to talk with you boys with the wings. When I see the Spitfires come over, I says to my mate, "Wish 'em luck. Hope they give Jerry hell."' 'Touch 'em George,' he said, pointing to the wings on the jackets, 'touch 'em for luck.'

About this time I saw 'Sailor' Malan at work. I never came to know him. His language over the RT they said, was distress-ful. But he re-formed his squadron at Kirton-in-Lindsay, and when they took off to go south again they took off on a grass aerodrome, twelve or fourteen Spitfires and every one in its proper place. I was impressed. Then we ourselves were sent to Gravesend; a small grass aerodrome south of the river, knee-deep in mud and innocent of any equipment whatever, save gooseneck flares and glimlamps.

By day, high-flying attacks were still being made on London, the condensation trails of attacker and defender powdered the sky far above us; by night, through the velvet darkness, searchlights and ack-ack pursued the raiders as they flew up the river. The ground would shake with the thud of the ack-ack, and in the sky were quick prickles of fire. The first maroon would sound at dusk, the all-clear would come again at dawn. It was November, and harsh winter winds chafed the estuary.

Frequently, we knew beforehand where the raid for that night would be. For early in the afternoon the Germans would lay a wireless beam over the target. The scientists would locate it. Group would ring us up by four o'clock. 'The raid is against Liverpool tonight, chaps,' or, 'The attack is going the other way.' We fumbled in the dark as best we might, but until we were re-equipped with twin-engined fighters and radar we could do little. Nevertheless, we learnt. We also had the doubtful satisfaction of being guinea-pigs on whom other people tried their inept ideas.

It was said that our esteemed Prime Minister visited the Fighter Command Operation Room in these early stages of the night attacks. Certainly, we were frequently in the air at times when we served more to encourage the civilians than to deter the Germans. England was burning, and something, it was supposed, must be done about it. The solution that we developed, as a result of our combined efforts, was that on moonlit nights the target area should be stacked with single-engined fighters, having only their eyesight to guide them; while the approaches to the target area should be covered by twin-engined fighters equipped with radar, working in conjunction with radar sets operating on the ground. By the middle of 1941, this system was in full force. But all during this winter, we struggled without radar and without the proper technique.

During one of many such patrols I made over London, that night the City, and Paternoster Row with all the books, and very nearly St Paul's went up in smoke. As the fire took hold, six of us were ordered off to patrol it, at heights ranging from fifteen to twenty thousand feet. There was little or no moon, a thick covering of cloud above us, with layers of stratus drifting in below upon an approaching storm. The blaze was going angrily when we arrived. It lit up a layer of cloud beneath us. Sticks of bombs would flash and flare as somewhere in the blackness a German aircraft tipped its load on to the flames. It was a stark occasion, but a fire, however great it be on the ground, gives off little light when you are three miles up. I banked and turned my small Hurricane in the darkness but I saw nothing against the rosy light of the flames; nor did any of us see each other, although we were only one thousand feet apart and patrolled the same spot. The weather deteriorated fast; it was that which saved the cathedral; for it was the German custom, when they had a good fire going, to load up again and double the attack before dawn. Their bases were in France, just across the Channel, so it was not difficult; and the burning city was the column of fire that went before them. The attack abated when rain closed down the aerodromes in Northern France, and friend and foe were content to land where they could.

I varied Air Force routine, as I was able, with a little poaching. Sammy Allard, at that time one of the top-scoring fighter-pilots, was a tough, able, unimaginative Yorkshireman with whom I frequently went shooting. It was never worthwhile hiring ground, for we moved too often from aerodrome to aerodrome. Instead, we shot over other people's estates, merely keeping our eyes skinned and rather shamelessly trusting that our exacting profession might keep us out of serious trouble. We shot the Isle of Sheppey in this way, always finding out the name of the owner of each farm. As there were no fences and no obvious boundaries, we could excuse ourselves by suggesting that we had mistakenly wandered from the next property, to which we had, of course, been invited. I pumped Sammy Allard about his fighting methods while we were drinking beer afterwards. He had stories to tell which were helpful to one who was still inexperienced. He told me how, after a skirmish over France, he had rejoined his flight, flying astern of the last aircraft. It suddenly dawned on him that they were Messerschmitts on whom he was flying; he had formed up on the enemy. 'To avoid suspicion I just followed them,' said Sammy, 'until we came past a convenient cloud.' From what he and others told me of their methods, I later came to believe that the Battle of Britain was won by fighter-pilots who had little idea how to shoot; and that the inability persisted in Fighter Command, certainly until well after the raid on Dieppe. The authorities then woke up to this flaw and began to take gunnery more seriously.

If there was a fatal weakness in Air Force thinking, it was this. Should a man be killed through what was termed enemy action, it was excusable and the fortunes of war. But, in fact, the opposite was true. Hard and proper training, I was convinced, joined to prudent leadership and methodical thinking, would avoid those deaths. Perhaps half the fighter-pilots who were killed never saw the aeroplane that destroyed them. Few fighter-pilots could shoot straight; whereas it was common to all the successful pilots of the previous war that they took infinite trouble over their guns and their target shooting. Then again, a pilot is half blind in an aeroplane because he is deaf, for, on the ground, our eyes are integrated with our ears. A pilot must always be searching and to do that with skill it is a question of knowing how to look as well as where to look. This is true by day or by night. It is a complete discovery, how to use sea, sun, moon, sky and cloud to ensure that you catch sight of the other man first, since every advantage falls to the pilot who sees without being seen. This much I began to learn, although it was another two years before I understood it properly.

Also, I found that the Royal Air Force had forgotten much of what was known in the previous war: to fight in large formations, to take gunnery seriously and to escort day-bombers with fighters – and had to re-learn these simple lessons painfully.

# Chapter 8

# Typical of Night-Patrolling

One sortie was much like another. Our whole squadron of eighteen pilots, toiling for six months, discovered but one German aircraft. It crossed the coast with its navigation lights on, hoping in that way to deceive the searchlights. So Peter Townsend shot it down.

On December 10th I made three patrols during the course of one night, finding myself getting very testy and short-tempered by the third.

An evening my wireless failed was fairly typical, and except for the failure, uneventful. We were short of pilots at the time, so I had two Hurricanes to look to – that meant two night-flying tests, two pleasant spells of aerobatics.

The long, minatory nose of a fighter-plane contained under the dun cowlings a Merlin engine, an instrument of precision, beauty and power. Upon the engine bearers rested a nation's intellect. And for the pilots, entrusted with this wonder, it spelt freedom. Freedom, it betokened, to zoom up to a great white cumulus, as the sun descended below the rim of the earth, a cumulus lit by its last rays, and to explore and to map and to project onto his forgetful mind, Xanadu shapes that would not last above five minutes. It spelt freedom to roll wildly and continuously among its snowy tops, to invert and dive ten thousand joyous feet down its sheer cliffs and then to climb back again, through more than Kubla Khan caverns, under huge overhangs, back to the last flush of daylight before the sun was finally dowsed. Cloud faces scaled in a matter of moments by swiftest rope climbers.

Great, ceremonious, passing day! Even as no two faces resemble each other, so, in their immensely greater proportion, no two days come near resembling each other; contiguous, they are related through an infinity of change in the microscopic parts, which brings about that vast alteration and pulsation of millennia of which this fading day was but a small, atomic particle and, at that, not the least. Our lives, marked out in days, are brief next to the annual pulse of a tree.

On one such lost winter evening, a stray Hurricane began to dog-fight with me. We wrestled with each other across the grey, snow-suggesting sky. We began head-on attacks. The Hurricane dived on me from above as I climbed up from below. Our closing speed must have been five or six hundred mph. At the last moment we both pulled away, but both to the same side. I thought a crash was unavoidable. As we passed, belly to belly, my aircraft was struck by something and I presumed my radiator had been removed. This was not the case but the air was compressed between our two airframes as we passed each other to such an extent that the bump from it had thrown my whole aircraft to one side. Two years later, again practising head-on attacks, I made the same error. They were narrower escapes than I cared for.

If you test an aircraft in the late afternoon, slow-rolling above the southern counties, London smoky in the distance, it is easy to believe that you can observe the rotundity of the earth. The fog of a winter day forms a curved band above the horizon, and the same frosty air that has cut back the vegetation to the ground, reaches to the stratosphere, growing ever colder with height. The sky is metal grey; and when a shade of blue is permissive, it is the lightest blue of an icicle.

I do not believe that any man, having grown into this hopeless winter world, is later unmarked. He is marked, not scarred. He is lifted out of the common philosophy; for such systems are set like Sheffield and Wolverhampton, between the narrow valleys of local presupposition. Rising above the winter weald, fields soft with snow, into the half-darkness of late afternoon, when ladies behind lace curtains have the light on and are taking tea, he is borne by a Rolls-Royce engine above the snow-clouds over the sad, winter sea.

Many of the great fear death. A pilot, who has faced death on many occasions, comes to be on a breezier footing both with this world and with the hereafter. The cold spaces are prophylactic. Much, therefore, that the world fears, I think he does not fear. He becomes for a season elemental, purged of all but the larger emotions. He grows attuned to sleet driving in from the sea.

But airmen, with many tales to tell, are mostly mute. Night falls; first upon the earth, then upon the sky. One star shone through the light cloud. We should have snow before midnight. 'Turn starboard, China one-eight, on to two-two-zero; bogey fifty miles south of you, believed coming north.'

'What height is he, Phosby?'

'I think about angels twenty.'

It is not always satisfying to kill a man you have never seen and would probably like, did you know him. Particularly when, as in my case, there were so many people I knew I would have happily destroyed. The grey scut of Dover was still visible. Expecting neither life after death, nor God in Heaven, nor greatness in victory . . .

'It is all right, China one-eight, it was a friendly.'

Darkness covered everything. The bleak December day had left us; the earth was obscured. At nineteen hundred revolutions, the engine had a certain suavity. The instruments were luminous and gave the only feeble light that glowed in the cockpit. The fish-tail exhausts spouted flame. A flicker of gunfire appeared in the distance; a flash and a momentary flame, two orange flares hung in the dark sky. The friendly appeared to have dropped bombs just the other side of the Channel.

Then the wireless went dead. When there is cloud above and below, as tonight, when there is no moon and only the occasional star visible, the wireless must fetch one home. I turned towards base, hoping for the best. The petrol tanks, I remember, showed about a quarter full. The night was sable.

Fortunately, the flashing beacon at Hawkinge showed up through a gap in the cloud. I reset the compass, and, boring through banks of cloud, headed towards base. Happily, they had coned the searchlights above base. I dropped down through cloud, just outside the balloon barrage, south of the river. The lights of Gravesend at seven hundred feet suddenly appeared, a row of handset glimlamps. Soon I was taxiing through slush and mud, the 'oleos' of the Hurricane clanking over the uneven ground. As I climbed out of the cockpit, dropping from the trailing edge into the puddled mire, the cold estuarine wind searched me, for all my padded clothing; wind off the November sea; sad world of white water, sandbank and whimbrel.

I did not desire, at twenty, to die; in truth I fought and struggled to live. But the notion came to me sometimes, facilely enough, that those who had had, not the ugly deaths but the quick and easy ones, were perhaps to be envied. One could never say.

# Chapter 9

# The Night Attacks – Spring, 1941

I was learning, along with everyone else, the martial virtue of patience. Queues, with especial secateurs, cut out a substantial portion from my life; they left a void in the day and in the personality. How many man-hours did I not annihilate among the cheap wood furnishings of orderly-rooms, standing patiently outside adjutants' offices, with the equipment clerks, filing first one form and then a second. It led to a vicious twist appearing in my character, as will the ill-treatment of an amiable dog. I did not conquer this worm that was eating into me before I had discovered that these grey, shuffling pauses in administrative blocks were ideal for self-education, so that I carried inside my uniform pocket a volume, the knowledge of which, I thought, would be necessary to me in later life, should I come through to see it. And it was so. Friends used to pass me, muttering: 'Sometimes oi sits and thinks and sometimes oi just sits.'

As to our flying business, 85 Squadron next moved to Debden, near Saffron Walden, in Essex. It was the squadron's peace-time station. Although German bombers had blasted the roofs off the aerodrome hangars, generally it was far more comfortable than our farm-house billet at Gravesend. About this time I met a friend from 264 Squadron. He told me that Basil Embry had replaced the old Squadron-Commander with a first-class man, 'Scruffy' Saunders, who, as I well recollect, used to keep his uniform trousers up with pyjama cord. Otherwise they also had been battling away with few results.

Then he told me of the death of 'Two-pint'. He was always called that – I forget his real name. He was Roddy Knocker's air-gunner. One night their aircraft caught fire in mid-air. Roddy crash-landed on the aerodrome, crawled out of the blazing cockpit and fainted. 'Two-pint' was trapped in the turret, unable to escape. The story as I was told it was this: two soldiers ran up, but because of the fierceness of the fire – and a burning fighter aircraft becomes a petrol-fired furnace in which belts of ammunition explode – they did nothing. I understand that they could see 'Two-pint' struggling inside his turret but that they were afraid, because of the flames, to help him. The doctor was rung up and informed of the accident. He had time to drive from the mess to the aerodrome, a distance of a mile or two, reach the crash, and pull the poor fellow out of the wreckage. In hospital he talked to his friends quite cheerfully and coherently although burnt to a cinder. He lived two days more.

Relatively, night-fighting was not a dangerous occupation. Risk came most often from engine failure, pilot error and weather. We had lost O'Malley in 264 from flying into the ground after take-off. In 85 Squadron, Pat Barclay, a likeable Irishman with a pleasing brogue, was shot down, and another sergeant, I forget his name, lost control of his Hurricane in bad weather and drove upside down into the ground.

Certain types of courage are common. When I had joined up I accepted the values people placed upon themselves. But as danger approached, they reacted differently; and in a way, the Air Force was a wonderful laboratory for the study of human character. We acquired ultimate truths about human beings. Those who failed earliest, it seemed, were the famous athletes, although of course there were gallant exceptions. The big imposing men, as a type, faltered next, burly fellows with big voices. One flight commander of my acquaintance – a strong fellow owning a big two-cylinder motorcycle – in place of taking off, during the Battle of Britain, sat back again and began to cry. Another strapping pilot won a VC. Having been awarded it, he refused to fly operationally again. The outstanding characters were of any sort and from any group. But the quality that mattered was spirit; and to my way of thinking the small insignificant clerk was the type that constantly emerged with flying colours. 'Two-pint' was such a one. He was even given that name, because, after two pints of diluted wartime beer, he was drunk. It was reported of him that he used to take the daily paper to read in his turret, in the belief that if there was anything to be seen, other people would see it first.

The top brass visited us at this time. They were not overwelcome to us since we came by high-sounding platitudes from them and we, in return, had perforce to sweep the locker room in order to receive them. Sholto Douglas came down in his magnificence and Sir Archibald Sinclair, the Air Minister, having first addressed us, left, waving his black Homburg hat theatrically in the air, with 'Goodbye and good hunting!' Lord Trenchard was simple and spoke to his youngesters as one man to another. Looking back at him now, from this distance of time, it would be true to say that he was as brilliant a creature as Nelson and a good deal more persistent. The Royal Air Force, like Nelson's navy, sufficed for one extended war only and died with its great organiser.

It was now early in 1941. Beaufighters, equipped with Mark IV Radar, were coming into service in increasing numbers, and with them German aircraft were more frequently destroyed at night. Furthermore, our fighters were crossing to France and destroying German bombers over their own bases. Our squadron was rearmed with Havocs, which were the Boston light bombers which had been first bought by the French and taken, I believe, to Martinique. Later fitted with eight guns in the nose (that sometimes ignited when you fired the gun), they were called the Havoc Night-Fighter and given to us. Things improved at once.

We started disastrously, however. Geoff Howitt, a sober, balanced Englishman if ever there was one, was addressing me in routine style on the shortcomings of the world in general and the Air Force in particular, as we stood on the steps of the Officers' Mess, when my shooting partner, Sammy Allard, took off from Debden in a Havoc. He had two other pilots in the plane, since they were to ferry other Havocs back from an aerodrome on the South Coast. One was a New Zealander known as 'The Ace', a highly successful pilot who called us all 'Cobber'; the second was Walker-Smith. Just after passing in front of us, the Havoc nose-dived into the next field, exploding on impact. We raced over; but there were only fiercely burning fragments of Duralumin left, the smell of burning flesh and that pall of black smoke which marks an oil fire.

Smoke from a chimney-stack, with its cowl for a draught, is a homely feature of town and country. The autumnal bonfire with the crackling as the twigs flare away, makes the English season, establishing it in our affections. But the black smoke rising from the oil fire of a crashed aircraft is harshly different. It is stridently etched into the view, its uncompromising blackness as it races heavenwards – for the heat of the blaze drives it skywards – is the flag and badge of death. With what a heavy and appalled heart have I not seen it, knowing that fellow pilots and close friends have been, were being or were about to be burned alive.

Within weeks success began to come to us, a new experience for a squadron that had toiled all winter to catch nothing. They gave me for my navigator, Harwood, a lad who had before been a professional dancing partner at the Nottingham Palais de Danse. He made a pleasant enough companion but his attention strayed rather to his peace-time work. We made contact in the early hours of the morning with an enemy bomber going out to sea. It was my first enemy contact at night. I closed in on him. There he was, a black stripe, opaque against the starlit night. His exhausts flickered. I raised the nose, aimed a little under him, since I was myself lower than he was, and fired three or four long bursts. He fired back, driving a hail of tracer all round us. I fired again, then my guns jammed. I broke away since I could not shoot. For ten minutes on my way back across the sea I was mute and unable to speak; for I had become so excited that the muscles proper for speech would not function, and try as I would to use the radio, nothing came of it.

We saw no results and we did not claim anything. The Armament Sergeant found that one gun had never fired, and the other seven had jammed for seven different reasons. The lesson that I learned was the danger of excitement. I decided that I must at all costs control my highly-strung self and become a precise, scientific craftsman; and this, so far as possible, I became.

Every good raid, someone scored. Geoff Howitt, vastly matter-of-fact, blew several bombers out of the sky. But before this run of success an event had occurred which rubbed salt into the wound of our previous failure. It was just before we finally gave up our Hurricanes. For I remember that I had been playing chess after dinner with the doctor, and later, drove round the perimeter track in my Morris 8 to 'B' Flight dispersal hut. As I did so, a twin-engined aircraft, showing navigation lights, turned into wind at the bottom of the runaway in use and took off. I thought no more of it. 'Nigger' Marshall, my Flight-Commander, Paddy Hemmingway the No 2 and several others were sitting round the clinker stove. There were Germans about; but the weather was indifferent and I was not due to be airborne before morning. A few minutes later the telephone rang. The control officers came through saying that the aircraft that had just scrambled was a Heinkel III. Apparently the pilot, after bombing one of the Midlands cities, had lost himself. He landed, thinking he was in France. One of the German crew climbed out, the telephone said, and went into the watch-tower, then became suspicious and ran for it. The control officer had seen the Teutonic crosses on the side of the plane but he had no gun; several army officers were present but they also were unarmed. The aerodrome defences, soldiers manning Bofors and Vickers guns, were not allowed to fire until they had permission from headquarters; and so, to make a long story short, the pilot took off and flew away. The Station-Commander, known familiarly as the Bulgarian General, received, it was whispered, a hard rap over the knuckles. But oh! the bitterness of it. We were consoled a little to hear later that the Heinkel had subsequently landed at a Bomber Headquarters in Cambridgeshire, and afterwards at Church Fenton in Yorkshire, before turning out to sea to go home.

At this time we moved to Hunsdon, a newly-constructed aerodrome in Hertfordshire. We retained the same sector.

Our mess was now a pleasant country house with a lake in front of it, and beside the lake stood a wood with a heronry, whose nests were built in the tops of pine trees. The cold nights were behind us. Violets had been appearing in the Essex hedgerows, and soon there was a nightingale singing nearby the dispersal hut. We had proper accommodation, an equipped aerodrome and warmer weather.

My own life had been changing. I had formerly been accustomed to walk by myself or with one other, whereas the pilots I was presently with, straggled untidily five or six in a group, down streets. They chattered about discs and women and their sentences were buttered with obscenities. I had undergone England's medieval schooling, which was arid and masculine; I had been with boys, not girls, and the general Christian ideal had been put over me that association with women had something wicked about it. Indeed, I had spent school holidays in fields and woods with a dog and had then found a spaniel and a scattergun sufficient company. Now my companions moved from the pub to the palais de danse and their erotic conversation proved strangely exciting and troublesome.

But before long I too was a dab-hand with the jargon and had the hang of it, able to release as round a string of oaths as the next man. Most young pilots started their flying careers as ingenuous as I; yet they, also, picked up the slang and it was we who became the bacteria to transform later pilots. I supposed aircrew were made a little like cheese.

I had changed my navigator for a soberer citizen, Smallie by name. We were on patrol one night, when he caught sight of a triangle of searchlights north of us. I asked and received permission to investigate it. Racing up there as fast as our Pratt and Whitney engines would take us, we picked up two contacts on the radar. I chose the one the searchlights were following, turned up behind it and saw a Ju 88. At the same moment I think a searchlight must have flicked over us, for he caught sight of us. It was approaching midsummer. There was no moon; but the sun moving from west to east below the horizon, at this altitude still rouged the sky to the north. Seeing us, our adversary dived into the dark, leaving us as we dived after him to stand out against the bright patch in the sky. A long stream of tracer came from him. I replied to his fire, but he was barely discernible in the darkness. He pulled out and flew level. Apparently travelling faster than him, we overshot, and flew parallel with him. I turned into him whereupon, quite rightly, he turned into me, passing just underneath me as he crossed, firing with his free gun at us but missing us at close range. I thought this to be a little one-sided, so I made a wide turn, picked up a contact and closed in upon it. It was one of our own fighters, we had changed to the second contact in the scrimmage. We did not see the Junkers again.

About this time there were changes in the squadron. Peter Townsend had put to a few of us in the bar one night, in his dry, nervous style, his belief that it was quite impossible to be both a good fighter-pilot and married. Within a short time he had announced his own engagement. Then he married – we formed a guard of honour for him – and he went for a rest. He had fought through the Fall of France and the Battle of Britain, and, in my experience, had steadily done two men's work in the arduous and at first unrewarding toil of creating England's night-fighter defences. He had devoted himself to building a great fighting formation, of which he would be the centre. He was, I think, completely exhausted and never flew operationally again. 'Nigger' Marshall, my Flight-Commander, an Englishman who had been brought up in West Africa, was sent to the first unit of flying-searchlights – of which more anon. He had been the CO's shadow, apeing his manner and copying his laugh. He soon killed himself with the flying-searchlights, squashing with half a ton of batteries into the ground, while showing off in front of his girlfriend, who watched him die. Paddy Hemmingway followed him on a rest, and I discovered, when I came back from leave, that Geoff Howitt and I had tossed a coin; I had lost, or so I was told anyway, and must go to the searchlights too.

I was sorry to leave the squadron. Imperceptibly I had grown accustomed to the nomadic existence. I still thought of myself as the Oxford student whom circumstances had forced into the Service; one who accepted the Air Force upon sufferance. But I had grown fond of my companions, and rather fonder of this wild life than I cared to admit.

There had been with us two entertaining French pilots, Labouchère and Fayolle, sons I believe of admirals who had been among the very few Frenchmen with the spirit to continue the war. They were both killed after leaving the squadron. James Wheeler, an ancient and experienced pilot who resembled a ship's figurehead, had vastly pleased us. He had been, I believe, too youthful for the previous war. So as a young man he had proceeded to a life of adventure, which included shearing sheep in Australia, before becoming a pilot on MISR Airways, the Egyptian Service. He was nearly always twice the age of his Commanding Officers. When they rated him for some error, he would gaze into their eyes and reply: 'What do you expect for 10/6d a day?' He enjoyed a paradox; fastening you with his steely pupils and pronouncing with unsmiling face the most improbable observations. We used to think he was a little nervous of being shot at by the Germans, having reached the age when caution becomes second nature. He rose quickly and deservedly. He professed not to want administrative work; so when they put him in command of Maidstone aerodrome, he ran it from the Star, the hotel in town, where we also had friends. Eventually he was killed commanding a Lancaster squadron.

James Wheeler, his navigator Charles Maton, and I used to play golf together at Saffron Walden. They chaffed me a good deal because I normally borrowed clubs, ball and tees, my brother having taken his own clubs to South Africa. Charles played an accurate game; indeed, I think he did most things well. The Germans eventually rescued him from the North Sea, after his squadron had been making torpedo attacks, if I remember the story, on a German convoy off Norway. They gave him two months' solitary confinement because they judged him, by his exalted rank for a gunner, to be a spy. Bill Carnaby later pulled a tail off a Mosquito and died that way. Another companion of that period, whether flesh or shade I do not know, was a shy, comely, russet-haired pilot called Sergeant Grey. He spoke with a gentle Derbyshire burr. He was a tiger for very low flying, and was accustomed to return, and get punished for it, with large pieces of tree rammed into his wing. Anyway, at this point I left them.

# Chapter 10

# The Airborne Searchlight

Summer, 1941, became all Chaucer and thinking. The wind swayed the long succulent grasses of the airfield. I remembered dozing thus, the year before, under an aircraft wing at Sutton Bridge, waiting to take my gunner to practise at a slieve, or the ground targets placed on Norfolk mud, or a sea-marker. Now 'Nigger' Marshall ran our new searchlight unit. There was little to do beyond the occasional flight, so I again lay in the sun, read books and enjoyed its warmth. It struck me, reposing thus, how little I needed for happiness: a friend; idleness in the countryside; sufficient to eat; the quiet following of my destiny. What bliss! To wake to idleness or to one's chosen work. I needed, I felt, only the sea and a sunburnt, happy companion with whom to play.

Why then, I asked myself, should I ever be corrupted to the appearance or to the actuality of business? If I survived, I might fear to fail at a great project and so would snatch at small success. I would not be, I knew, as independent of the world in practice as I was free in theory; when she spoke strongly to me I might listen. The fleshpots of the world had no great hold over me, but the Puritans, with their word 'duty', might trap me.

I had emulated a dead friend by keeping a small library with me on each aerodrome. I endeavoured to educate myself, ever more persistently as the war years rolled by. I became interested in limits, a challenging and arresting expression. The confines men may not pass: Keep off the grass! Ladies! Do not spit! The convention of what you may or may not do seemed to me to be mistaken by the masses for natural law. It struck me that if Nature herself, whom poets in every Golden Treasury carol, were to appear in person in England she would be gaoled for indecency. Not that the young were prudish, but later the old wear prudery to make a virtue of their looks.

I wished to enquire further, into the *flammantia moenia* of the mind, the reason why man raises one question and not another, failing to observe alternatives. It was the certainty with which intelligent men raised a false disjunction that alarmed me. All atoms, they proposed, were identical; forgetting that, to a foreigner, all Chinese look alike.

The limits! The limits of daring! The limits of sympathy! The lack of communication between the bomb-aimer and the bombed! I had yet to find one who, though a good man, felt more sympathy for Judas than for his Lord. The limits of action and of admission!

Our belief in personal identity imposes restrictions. If you held that each one of us was governed by an imperceptible and immortal soul, then this identity is understandable. I did not. Despatch this soul and you enfranchise the individual, for he no longer need be on Thursday the same man as on Tuesday. He has habits which may be broken and memories to be forgotten. Of course his friends do expect consistency in him and this tends to make him consistent.

It is the common error in each period to believe that we are at the end of human progress, that we have reached a peak of development, or that the future would only hold more of the same sort of thing. Thus Lucretius saw his own day; so Comte characterised the history of mind. He did not see that the Scientific spirit is itself limited, and would be replaced, I thought, by Creativity. For we seemed already to be primarily interested in making things, thereafter we studied what we had made. And the whole universe was our raw material. And if the intellect was in its infancy, so also was love and the other emotions.

So I looked to the adventure of the Air Force, if I could only survive it, as a diversion from the greater speculative adventure that would be my peace-time career, if I had the ability to make it so.

After a few days of this rest, I sickened. The flying searchlight, or Helmore, was a Boston containing in its bomb-bays half a ton of batteries. The nose was a searchlight; and the glass face of it being flat the aircraft wandered even on the calmest days. It was illogical equipment. For if radar could take you to a thousand yards of the target, it could take you the next eight hundred. Once the range was closed, we could always see our targets by the glow of their engine exhausts, however dark the night. On moonlit nights you could see a thousand yards anyway; and on dark nights, which were most frequently cloudy, the difficulty of keeping two aircraft in close formation was excessive, for the Helmore needed another fighter to fly with it, which at the proper time could go forward into the glare to shoot the bombing aircraft down. I believe that someone had sold this foolish idea to the Prime Minister. Now that a new formation was to come into being, many officers saw promotion in it for themselves, and however wrong the scheme, were tempted to support it. I wrote a three-line letter to the group officer in charge of postings, saying that I thought the Helmore to be a retrograde step, a waste of time and money and I asked to be posted to a proper formation. It turned out that Peter Townsend was that officer. He fortunately saw the humour of this letter and arranged my exchange with one Curtis, a mature pilot of 264 Squadron, also due for a rest.

At this time, inventiveness was to the fore. That ancient innovator, Pemberton Billing, held forth in the Press that what England required was not a blackout but a light-up. The country, he said, must be fully illuminated, so that the boys might see the raiders against an incandescent England. Lord Cherwell had conceived Operation 'Pegasus'. This involved the laying of aerial mines in the path of the raiders. The mines, I think, were chunks of old iron suspended from a parachute; and in the final part of their descent, used to sweep away with them all the high-tension cables and telephone wires in that neighbourhood. The Admiral paced his bridge, the Senior Air Force Officer stayed on the ground; and being a war out in his experience, often lacked the precise feel of the material he was using.

At one time the aircrew were adjured to wrap their lunches in a paper-bag and eat with the labourers working on the aerodrome, to exhort them to work harder. In reply, we suggested more direct encouragement. Then they gave us pink pills to improve night vision; which were said, among the more licentious, to give you wet dreams in Technicolor. Then, after the doctors had made detailed tests on carrots, pink pills, and other aids to night vision, a paper was circulated which admitted all these aids to be useless, except, a rather lame paragraph admitted, for a small quantity of alcohol, which for a brief period stimulated it.

I exchanged places with this older pilot, Curtis. He took over my navigator, Smallie; I took over his gunner. Curtis had been with 264 Squadron above a year, had two or three of the enemy to his credit, and I judged him rather more likely to survive than me. In the event, he killed himself and my navigator soon afterwards. With great spirit, Smallie's wife replied to the unit commander's condolences, saying that she too would like an opportunity to fly in a night-fighter. Curtis was an interesting person. Before the war, he had served, so he said, in the Foreign Legion. He joined the RAF as an air-gunner, and had trained as an air-gunner at Aston Down when we were all there, including some of the gunners still present in the squadron. He had flown privately before the war. At some point after Aston Down, so these gunners swore, he wrote his log-book up himself and joined the squadron as a pilot. It was a remarkable instance of the truth that brass is nearly as good currency as gold. To begin with, when he was lost on a cross-country path, he used to drop down to an aerodrome, and find out where he was by referring to the address on the note-paper in the Officers' Mess. But he had long grown accustomed to piloting, had a wonderful presence of mind in an emergency and, as I say, had shot down two or three German aircraft during the previous year by attacking them as they came in to land at their own aerodromes in Northern France. So he went to safety and a rest, and I rejoined my old fighter squadron, gratefully.

# Chapter 11

# The George And Dragon

Every squadron annexed a pub; from Duxford it had been the Red Lion at Trumpington. What huzzahs there were, when, long afterwards, it was reported that mine hostess bore a child with red hair! At Caistor, the waterlogged satellite of Kirton-in-Lindsay, there was a telephone tie-line between the nearest pub and the airfield. If you claimed that the weather was unflyable you were compelled to wait for it to clear; but if you could put the aerodrome unserviceable, which we frequently did, you would be undisturbed for the rest of the night. From West Malling, where 264 now resided, we took over the George and Dragon. I came into the picture long after their occupation was complete.

My first night on the squadron, when I was feeling delighted to be back, we retired there; and several friends 'genned' me up with all that had happened since I left. For I had been away nine months and much had occurred in that time. Desmond Hughes had continued to do well. Roddy Knocker had been shot down over London by our own ack-ack. He had baled out; and my old colleague, Hardie, who was by then Roddy's gunner, had broken his legs on the tail-plane when abandoning the aircraft. One of the pilots had lost his nerve and been killed, another had been pitched out of the squadron and I think the Air Force.

My chief informant was an Administrative Officer. He was later to join Mountbatten's staff in the Far East; thence to return in irons with a sentence of twelve years, convicted of swindling an Indian out of £100,000. Now, however, he was in his element; for he wagged an amusing and wicked tongue and had made shrewd study of the pilots.

The first tale concerns 'the Mouse'. The Mouse was a professional officer, who owned a fast sports car and a large moustache; and appeared to me to be drained of both physical and mental strength. Someone had advised the Mouse to look to his future after the war. He must begin now to consider what line of business he would take up, and come to know something about it. The Mouse must have taken this conjuration seriously. The facts leaked out when he asked to borrow £10 from Tommy, the Flight-Commander of 'B' Flight. The latter was a valiant Welshman, the very stuff of which the Royal Air Force was made, who was later shot down and made a prisoner while leading a squadron of Typhoons. The enterprise was this:

The Mouse had been drawn into conversation with a tart in Piccadilly, who had suggested to him that they go into business together. All that she required, she stated, was £20 in order to furnish a room and thereafter they would cut fifty-fifty. The Mouse carried his cheque-book with him, so there and then he wrote out for her a cheque comprising his entire wealth. She told him that she would meet him outside Lyons Corner House at 10 o'clock the following morning in order to show him her apartment. Of course he waited; but she had cashed his cheque and vanished.

The second tale concerned a smash on the flare-path at Luton. It ran something like this: James Melville, a fat, good-natured Wykehamist with a taste for beer, had just landed his Defiant. In place of turning off the flare-path, he taxied down it, which we often did in those days. For obvious reasons we carried no navigation lights. Bowen at that moment took off, and hit the taxiing aircraft when he had himself just attained flying speed, which was about 100 mph. No one was killed, but everyone, except for Bowen's gunner, Stephen Hill, was burnt or seriously injured. Stephen's turret broke away from the aircraft with him in it. A soldier ran to the rescue, seized an axe, struck a blow through the glass of the turret to release Stephen who was trapped inside, and caught him a nasty blow on the head. Now Stephen was always eccentric. He was a first-class shot with rifle and shotgun, a good bridge player and a great airgunner. But he was an excitable cove. One night, when Defiants were attacking aerodromes in France, his turret had jammed. The German ground-control, believing them to be a German aircraft, had flashed permission to land, whereupon Stephen implored his pilot to accept this permission and to let him jump out to cut the throats of anyone he could find. Another time, after a beer party, he was to be found on the roof of the Officers' Mess, without shoe or sock, hurling slates at any officer who tried to enter. He told a story of how he rode the unridable mule at Olympia. In short, he won his £5 for doing so but his hospital fees arising from the kicks amounted to £150. However, the point is this: the medical authorities had written to our Commanding Officer for permission to certify Stephen as insane, while the former had ignominiously to reply that they should do no such thing – he was always thus.

The George and Dragon was kept by May and Dora; respectively the comfortable elderly hostess and her boss-eyed daughter. 'Time gentlemen please!' May sang out; and with a nod and a wink, motioned her Air Force boys into the back-room. When the general public had left, and the blinds had been drawn and the windows shuttered against the police, we came back into the bar. Only this time May perched on one man's knee, Dora an another, two of the lads went behind the counter, Hugh Percy broke into the poor-box for further monies and the party warmed up, continuing thus until dawn.

I came to believe at this time that, substantially, there are no vices. I held the liveliest recollection of hell-fire sermons, the awe-inspiring horror with which certain actions were invested by the church. I discovered that there were tricks which were silly and childish and some that were delicious; none that I found equalled in damage the sermons themselves or deserved supernatural terror. It is the declaimer, customarily, who is sick. I think that my fellows went through the most cheerful actions almost in innocence. Happiness lies in holding a proper balance between squalor and respectability. It is found in inverse proportion to hygiene.

# Chapter 12

# Is Courage Cumulative?

Is courage cumulative? When seamen perished, did all their courage die with them, wash away with them? Did Stone-Age man, through his hundreds of thousands of years, suffer for himself alone, privately, and to give only a physical birth to a later age? Or are our courage and cowardice largely derived from our parents and the whole a spiritual accumulation of half a million years? Pilots fought, in the main, from self-respect. Does that term admit a linkage, however subconscious, between ourselves and the greater generations before and behind? I felt that it was so but I was not sure of it.

But certainly there was a quality to a pilot's courage that is not often touched upon. For the Air Force had a seamy side of which the flying crews were dimly aware. It was the misfortune of the Royal Air Force that only a very few of its people took the air and came into danger, the administrative officers in particular remaining securely on the ground. A handful of these administrative officers would be suspected of illicitly selling Air Force equipment and stores, and in the later stages of the war, looting in one form or another. Stories would be bandied around about this. So that while the younger men were daily risking their necks, a very few of the older ones were making money, sometimes on quite a scale. This gave rise to the notion that war encouraged the exploitation of the young by the old, a notion that was not altogether foolish.

Slowly I discovered the people in adversity to be more congenial than in good fortune. For in adversity their outer pretences were down and I met the actual individual, often warm and sensitive. By comparison, how uninteresting was the box at the theatre and the expensive lunch!

Flattery was by rank. 'Erks' evinced so little desire for promotion it was hard to maintain the establishing of NCOs. I found aircrew normally as unambitious until they reached a senior grade. For it was senior officers whom the glitter of gold braid seduced; they began to flatter their immediate superiors, massaging their egos like an ant going to work on a greenfly. Observing it quietly in the mess, I found it a little unpleasant. In some cases, for I was still young and unforgiving, the motorcycle escort of power looked not to be the aura of greatness but the perimeter defence of littleness. A big man is usually simple. As a cynical youngster, stripes seemed to me to be all too frequently the bow-waves painted upon a destroyer to give a deceptive illusion of speed. Or, to take the marine parallel further, these men were the *Marie-Celeste* that sailed across the ocean, all her canvas stretched, but there was no one aboard.

I was swopping discoveries in these matters one night with a friend in Ruskington. We had made our way through the blackout towards the Leg of Mutton. The cars which slooshed past us in the rain had their lights so dimmed they served no better than the white walking sticks of blind men. The pub door hinged open to reveal a bar three deep in aircrew. The electric light dazzled me after the dark. We hit a fug of tobacco smoke. Some few grey civilians had been elbowed into corners, where they stood talking quietly to each other, while the flying-crews, with shoulder-flashes from half the world, jawed, flushed and exuberant.

These were mostly bomber crews and my companion, Johnny, who was one of their number, looked at me seriously and imparted to me in a whisper that a certain barmaid was reputed to be a spy, so that the Germans mostly knew in advance where the RAF would be raiding. A Canadian acquaintance lurched over to us. 'Have you heard this one, Johnny?' he asked and began to tell us how a pilot walked into the mess on a strange station and ordered himself a drink. As he looked at the other types in the room, he picked out faces he had not seen for some time. While he was raising his drink a strange thought troubled him – the penny dropped – all these men were dead. The Canadian looked at me seriously, raised a non-existent cap and went through the motion of digging.

# Chapter 13

# 264 Squadron: West Malling

It was not easy at this time to look ahead. Only the Commonwealth was fighting Germany. Although we had repelled the daylight attacks upon England and were now able to shoot down a percentage of the night-bombers sent against us, there seemed no chance that by herself the Commonwealth could knock out an embattled Europe, with its systems of slave-labour in the munition factories, its conscripted armies, the rule of terror; the whole Nazi army backed by the tacit or active assistance of multitudinous Russians. We had been thrown out of Greece and Crete, snubbed in Africa. For my part, I looked ahead for a brief week or so, no more; indeed, no further dare a fighter-pilot look. For the future that opened up before me promised only many, many years of fighting, and that being the case, there seemed little weary chance that any of us would survive it.

We had with us in the squadron a certain noble peer descended from the conqueror of India, Clive. He was immensely tall, burly with it and older than he should have been for our profession. He was a good man, but a bad pilot; handicapped because he was forced to hibernate through the winter by reason of sinus trouble. His manner of speech and peculiar jests were parliamentarian. I recollect him spending one evening explaining to a young girl of fairly easy virtue the finer points of chemical warfare. On occasion, he used to seek and obtain permission to absent himself from us for part of a session, and then hitch-hike his way to the House of Lords. 'The Germans attacked Russia this morning,' he told me. We discussed this portentous event; and with that discussion, then hope flickered for the first time. For the old Napoleonic strategy was repeated; and I could dimly see how, in combination with Russia, victory might be won at some measurable period in the future. This was the most encouraging tidings of the war.

The armies that rolled into the Soviet Union that dawn stretched for sixteen hundred miles. Field Marshal Mannerheim, and his revengeful Finns attacked across the tundra in the north, two million Germans thrust through the centre. Hungarians, Bulgarians, Italians and Rumanians joined with the Germans in the south. Hitler's *grande armée*, innumerable in tanks and warplanes, advanced upon Moscow. We know now that the Russian peasants first welcomed them as liberators. But when the insane murder squads followed behind the troops, they turned about. One hundred and fifty million Russians were left no choice but to fight to the death. Between the butcher, Stalin, and the butcher, Hitler, they opted for Stalin. So deeply did the Germans plunge, their bomber force could never again be spared to attack England in any strength. That to us was the outcome of that fateful morning.

We shared West Malling aerodrome with 219 Squadron. Her pilots were equipped with Beaufighters carrying Mark IV Radar. We flew our Defiants and for our results were compelled to rely upon the naked eye. There remained sufficient German activity, chiefly mine-laying in the Thames Estuary, to keep 219 Squadron busy; and as they were properly equipped, the best opportunities were given to them. We patrolled, practised, trained, and attempted to guard the Channel ports.

Bob Martin was the name of Curtis's gunner whom I took over when we exchanged. He was a quiet, self-possessed person. He had been a Lieutenant-Colonel in the infantry at one time, during the First World War, and so was a long way above the average age of air-gunners. Before the outbreak of this war he had worked in the teak industry in Burma. Then he went to 85 Squadron as an Intelligence Officer. He related to me with much humorous detail, how he was instructed by the Air Ministry during the fighting in France, to take scrapings of paint from the wings of those Hurricanes which had flown through the German vapour trails. It seemed that in those early days of the war, the phenomenon was not understood, being mistaken for gas.

I knew that I grew too excited when there was a chance of combat, so I judged it to be particularly fortunate to have as my gunner a man at once so able and mature. I thought he would steady me down. Of course he did no such thing. Indeed, I soon discovered him to be more excitable than me. There developed an attack upon Dover one night when our IFF, a wireless recognition signal, failed. It was a clear night with a half moon. Divebombers were crossing the Channel – that was lead inset with a thin strip of silver for the moon's path – dropping their load of bombs onto the small, balloon-protected port. When we approached Dover, the English shot at us, near Calais, the Germans shot at us, and as we patrolled a narrow passage between, a twin-engined aircraft passed ahead of us, flying at speed towards Belgium. I pursued as I could, but before I could identify it, and without being given permission to fire, Bob Martin opened up and sent a stream of pink night-tracer past the intruder. The aircraft turned, and as I saw its silhouette against the moon's silver path along the sea, I recognised it for a Beaufighter.

'Fired your guns, Sir?' the armourer asked Bob as soon as the prop stopped after landing back. I was myself anxiously speculating how to explain this gaffe away. 'Fired a practice burst, Corporal,' he replied. Next morning I received a little note from the Commanding Officer, obliging us, when we tested the guns, not to burn so much ammunition. Our target had been Bob Braham, a Flight-Commander of 219 Squadron, a good friend of mine and one of the leading Allied night-fighter pilots.

After the big attack on London, in May of 1941, the German bomber force was withdrawn from the Western to the Russian front and never came back in any strength. Our own night-fighter squadrons continued to improve in skill and equipment, becoming, partly because casualties were relatively low, one of the most highly trained and scientific groups in the Royal Air Force. As things turned out, it was only in aggression that their abilities were fully used; either covering the invasions of North Africa, Italy and Normandy, or escorting the night-bomber force across the Ruhr. Due to the Russians, we now ran out of Germans. But the war might have gone very differently.

As a result of this quietness, Bob Martin became restive. He and Stephen Hill decided that for further experience they would take their leave on a bomber squadron, so when I went home for a week's leave, they joined a squadron in Cambridgeshire which flew four-engined Stirling bombers. Stephen's aircraft was attacked by German fighters, and from such an angle that he was unable to bring his guns to bear. His excitement and frustration mounted so high that he burst a small blood-vessel and was unable to fly again for a month. On Bob Martin's first trip, his Stirling had hydraulic trouble, so they returned to the aerodrome and crash-landed. From his second raid, the aircraft never returned. Friends told me later that they thought he preferred to die.

In December, I was offered the job of Flight-Commander on 125, Newfoundland Squadron. The Squadron-Commander was a friend from 264 Squadron, a gentle, old womanish pilot known to his associates as 'Auntie B'. The squadron was stationed on the Fairwood Common aerodrome, near Swansea, in Wales. I accepted this offer and arrived there on New Year's Day, 1942.

# Chapter 14

## 125 Squadron: The Air-Gunners Posted Away and Killed

War helped me to understand. For although I lost six or seven years of study to flying, and half my physique, I was given in their place a perfect setting in which to curiously observe my friends. It seemed to me that only a scholar and a recluse could hate humanity, and indulge in that grand general distaste for the human race that a few acquaintances professed. For when I was feeling most cynical, empty and bitter – a mood that overtakes most people I suppose at one time or another – some perfect stranger would do me unlikely kindness: an old cockney dame would press a cup of tea upon me; a ticket-collector warmly refuses to accept his fare, or some such. They would be trivial things in themselves; I think they affected me by their unexpectedness.

Sometimes, I felt myself to have little in common with other pilots. But occasionally, too, I found a kindred spirit from whom I could learn a great deal.

I had come to believe by now, that given some sort of horizon to the night sky, a fighter could be manoeuvred as ruthlessly by night as by day; and I intended to impress upon my flight in 125 Squadron the skills I had learnt from the Hurricane pilots. In return, I enjoyed the pleasantest companionship I have ever known and they, for their part, taught me a great deal about human decency. It was my first command and with it I found myself.

Now not only were they pleasant people in themselves, but

they lived then, I fancy, at a higher pitch than they will ever live again, at least those among them who survived – and a number did. For there was nothing personal we could gain by success, save a ribbon and rank; and I do not think we cared too much about either. There is nothing petty about the air; and the loudest-mouthed, once he was off the ground, had no better chance of surviving than anyone else.

Like many another pilot, I was beginning to show the strain physically, for the degree to which I had to drive myself to the job was beginning to tell. My hand shook. I carried tea-cups tilted to one side to conceal the rattle. An eyelid twitched and my heart fluttered alarmingly. When I ran out at night to take off, I hiccuped or belched. But once in the cockpit and the throttle open, it was all forgotten; gone the shaky hand, the twitch, the belch, the heart-flutter, only excitement and professional skill and the brine of the winter night.

In contrast to our work, we enjoyed a pleasant, uninhibited existence when off duty. Pilots preserved a resource which I always admired, counting it in fact above most other virtues. For instance, I was sitting in a café in Saffron Walden one morning in the spring of 1941, with a scarred pilot of 85 Squadron called Gus Gowers, whose face had been burnt and had since refleshed. He came, as we constantly reminded him, from the village of Steeple Bumpstead. Two old ladies came to our café table. They said simply: 'We want to thank you for protecting us.' My education had been much too good to leave me anything else than tongue-tied. Gus, otherwise something of a nitwit, at once responded, saying in a pretty speech, that it was really nothing at all and that we enjoyed doing it anyway.

Another time Thomas, the solid Welsh Flight-Commander of 264 Squadron, distinguished himself. Boulton and Paul, manufacturers of the Defiant, gave our squadron a party of heroic proportions to celebrate its hundredth victory. Our score had refused to budge from ninety-seven, but we were not particular. The aircrew were taken to Wolverhampton and wined and dined by the firm. So liberally, in fact, were we plied with beer, there was always three pints in front of us at dinner. As one was consumed, another was brought up.

After dinner came a show. For each of us a factory girl was provided for company; and all would have been well, had not the flow of beer grown so excessive, that there was never above half the aircrew in their seats. Boulton and Paul were a firm of importance to Wolverhampton: and they arranged for the show to be stopped and the comedian to patter: 'We have with us here in the house, etc, . . .' Then we were told to go on stage. But no one was in his chair. When I came in I glanced down a long row of alternate girls with empty places beside them. Eventually half a dozen of us were impressed and pushed onto the platform. At this crisis in our existence, Flight-Commander Thomas took control; and, whatever his own needs, thanked all and sundry for their kindness with military composure and absolute propriety.

Another more lively incident occurred later. Harry was an Australian. He had left Nottingham at the age of twelve, and in his eight years in the Antipodes had become even more Australian than the rest of them. He was short, young and cocky. 'We were in a pub in London,' Jerry said, 'when a Canadian soldier, about twice Harry's size, picked on him and told him to come outside. Harry shuts his eyes and gropes his way to the door. The massive Canadian follows. We hear a crack. Poor Harry, we lament, poor, poor Harry. In comes Harry, grinning all over his face and blowing on his knuckles. He had just shut his eyes to grow used to the darkness, walked out, framed the Canadian against the light of the pub door when he left and knocked him out.'

I reached Fairwood Common to find that 125 Squadron was but recently formed, and that all the pilots had newly finished their training. Furthermore, we were shortly to be rearmed with Beaufighters. I was given 'A' Flight, and Desmond Hughes arrived soon after to take over 'B' Flight. From Swansea where we were, we were supposed to protect the heavy industry of South Wales, and to do what we could for the convoys that mustered in Milford Haven, or passed through the Bristol Channel and the Irish Sea. There was little enemy activity; the Germans occasionally attacked ships at dusk and we suspected them, probably falsely, of lining up seaplanes by the Saltee Islands for their purposes.

When we went to Colerne, which we moved to in February 1942, all the gunners were posted off to Bomber Command, and with few exceptions were straight-way killed, for Bomber Command was taking heavy punishment at this time. The best example was Tom Delaney, a cheerful Newfoundlander. He left Swansea in the afternoon and joined his new squadron, armed with Bostons, at 11 o'clock the next morning. They were flying off an aerodrome on the East Coast. He was given no time for lunch, nor to become acquainted with his guns. Instead, they packed him into the back of a Boston as soon as he arrived, which was forthwith shot down into the Channel, where he was drowned.

Another who died was Johnny Sharpe. He was a shy, reticent lad, nineteen or twenty years old; fair; very handsome and as I think often happened with the reticent ones, an adventurer. He became tail-gunner in a Wellington; and, so my informant assured me, did not give a damn for anything. One night he forgot the breech-blocks for his guns (I think that was the part that was missing) and only discovered his slip when they were half-way over Germany. They were attacked by a German night-fighter. Johnny was stuck out at the tail-end of the aircraft with nothing he could do. However, after a great struggle, they eluded their adversary. The crew completed their tour, made one last unnecessary sortie, and have never returned from it.

My predecessor in 125 Squadron, 'Connie', had been posted to the Far East. He left behind him an address list of his girlfriends and an airgunner, whom I also inherited. 'Torchy' Blain was thin, wizened as a grenadilla, and one of the kindest, most generous souls ever born. Before the war he had drifted about the world; his previous occupation was gold-prospecting in East Africa. He never had money, for as soon as there was anything in his pockets he had found means to give it away. 'Nobody above the rank of Flight-Lieutenant,' he complained, 'is worth talking to.' Torchy refused to train as a radar operator 'squinting down miserable little tubes' but instead left for Bomber Command, where he was immediately killed. In this swift way our gunners perished.

# Chapter 15

# Baedeker Raids Against Bath

We re-equipped with Beaufighters fitted with Merlin engines. They were inclined to swing badly on take-off and landing; while their engines, being rated for about eighteen thousand feet, left us seriously under-powered near the ground. When we took off at night, we struggled to climb over the chimney stacks and the roofs of the houses, for it was difficult to attain single-engined flying speed. This gave me a curiously unpleasant feeling, but in the event the engines proved wholly reliable. Thanks to the caution of our engineering staff, we never had trouble from them.

With the extra equipment and the increased size of the maintenance staff, higher-ranking officers were brought in. Eric Barwell became a Flight-Commander, Desmond Hughes and myself were made No 2 in our respective flights. They put over me a middle-aged regular; a hard, humourless Scot whose previous experience had been thirteen years in training command. I disliked him for his lack of courage and of ability; and following the principles which I earlier adumbrated, told him so and so met trouble.

At that time I became increasingly interested in the two deaths men die, the death of the integrity and the death of the body. And even where the integrity had not altogether perished, the restriction of personality. For when I was eight, so it seemed to me, everything was then open to me that could be encompassed by a healthy male; my limitations were then elemental – now they were become physical.

For I was already confined at the age of twenty-two, by what I knew, or did not already know. My brain was a junkshop of useful knowledge. I could ride a motor cycle, half read French, discover wild-fowl, fly an aeroplane, make some small use of Latin. One parasang is equal to three miles. And by this encyclopaedia I was constrained. It led me to persons and places, it elbowed out the new, it suppressed music.

Conversely, I could hardly now become a great draughtsman, a violinist, or a ballet-dancer. The passion of the Romeo was beyond me; not perhaps for strength but for novelty, although I might hanker after a sepia beauty, or a Danish girl with hair of whipped ivory. I could no longer find in a foreign country the romance that I once did – for nationalism is heavenly that so aids the imagination. Some novelties had departed forever.

I love a child, partly for the mystery of what the child can become. Possibility is the divine spark. I dislike those adults who have become all that they can become, and have then spiritually withered and perished. For the first death is the death that shall be wept; the second death is but the lying-in-state, the waxing and the interment of a corpse that had for long been both existent and perished. There are degrees of life as there are degrees of courage and of understanding. The first death comes early; for few survive their call-up and conscription into society.

Nothing much happened at Colerne, save the Baedeker raids against Bath. During the first attack I was on a routine patrol over the Irish Sea. I was told nothing of the raid, being held over the western patrol line above a path that was not used that night, while other fighters were called up from the ground to deal with the emergency. Only on my return did I see the fires burning in the city, and switching radio channels, impatiently discover that the raid was completed.

Ivins, our new Squadron-Commander, wisely decided that the Germans might repeat their attacks, since in their reprisal raids on the other historic towns, they had done just this. So 'B' Flight brought the old Defiants back from retirement and stood by to do a fighter cover above the city, for there was enough moonlight. 'A' Flight continued with the new Beaufighters. I was again on patrol and had this time arranged that I was in no circumstances to be left out in the cold if a raid should develop. I was up at twenty thousand feet, the empty night sky brilliant and fleecy – but nothing came of it. An hour after my patrol was complete and I had landed, the expected raid began. They were short, swift raids at this time, using fifty aircraft. It was not my turn to take off; and while the raid developed on Bath, which was but five miles distant, three or four of us waited on the ground with great impatience. The Germans began to machine-gun our aerodrome. Then I was ordered off. The flare-path had been extinguished, and the officer in charge was lying under the floodlight, doubtless offering up prayers. The runway was short for our aircraft but I could discern part of its outline in the moonlight and was just turning to take off when, in the gloom, I misjudged the end of it and wrapped myself in the barbed-wire defences of the airfield. Bombs were dropping nearby, flak was climbing up into the night, German tracer was criss-crossing the aerodrome, searchlights were swinging about the sky, none of the props for a spectacular raid was missing, and I was stuck in the fences, helpless, a snared partridge.

Ivins was a genuine and sincere man, a regular with the interest of the Air Force much at heart. He had recently taken me into his office to complain that I treated the Air Force like a flying club, to which he added, more in sorrow than in anger, that I walked around the aerodrome like a shepherd. We had learnt that he had met with a severe accident early in his flying days, as a result of which he invented the quick-release clip to the safety straps. He had also been trepanned. The engineering officer used to suggest, when he ran foul of him, that the pan was rusting. And that was my feeling during the next weeks. For I could not work with my Scot – Desmond Hughes also

## LICENCE AIR

Photograph     of Holder.

Signature of Holder.....*C.R.A. Bailey*.....................

This Pilot's Licence for private flying machines

No.........19725..........................................................dated

..............20th July, 1939..........has been issued to

.............J.R.A. Bailey................................................

who is hereby licensed to fly the following types
of flying machines :—

        All types of landplanes.


This licence is valid.......See page 4................

Given at.............London.........this.......20th.....day

of.................July..........19 39.

*S.W.Warden*

*for*

*Director of Home Civil Aviation.*

*Above: The prototype Boulton and Paul Defiant, which flew forwards and shot backwards.*

*Below: 85 Squadron's Christmas card for 1940, showing a flight of Peter Townsend's Hurricanes. When I commented that the card wasn't very Christmassy I was howled down – I hadn't done the work.*

'A' Flight, 125 Newfoundland Squadron. From left to right: Jamie Mathews, Johnny Surman, Adjutant Morgan, (?), me with spaniel Juno, Bill Williams, 'Jesus' Morgan, Johnny Sharpe, Dicky Bastow, Williams, 'Tickey', Brem Lacy with dog Andy, Newton, White.

*St. Paul's Cathedral during the night bombing when I was one of the six Hurricanes patrolling the fire.*

*The rugby team of the bomber aerodrome of Marston Moor,*
*Yorkshire, winter 1944. I am in the back row, fourth from*
*the right.*

| Rank | | No. 264 Squadron | | | Plt.Off. | W.A. | Ponting | C Killed * |
|---|---|---|---|---|---|---|---|---|
| 1940 | | During The Battle of Britain | | | Sgt. | L.A.W. | Rasmussen | C Killed * |
| Sgt. | R.T. | Adams | | C Killed | Plt.Off. | G. | Robinson | C |
| Sgt. | M.R. | Andrews | | C Died | Sgt. | L.P. | Russell | C |
| Flt.Lt. | R.C.V | Ash | | C Killed * | Sgt. | W. | Scott | C |
| Plt.Off. | J.R.A. | Bailey | | | Fg.Off. | J.G. | Shaw | Killed * |
| Sgt. | B. | Baker | | C Killed * | Sgt. | F.W. | Shepperd | C Killed |
| Flt.Lt. | A.J. | Banham | | | Plt.Off. | L.W. | Simpson | C |
| Sgt. | F.J. | Barker | | C | Sgt. | G.E. | Smith | C. Died |
| Plt.Off. | E.G. | Barwell | | | Fg.Off. | D.M.A. | Smythe | C |
| Sqn.Ldr. | L.G. | Belchem | | Killed | Fg.Off. | I.R. | Stephenson | Killed |
| Sgt. | A. | Berry | | C Killed * | Plt.Off. | R.W. | Stokes | Killed |
| Plt.Off. | F.D. | Bowen | | Killed | Plt.Off. | A.J. | Storrie | C Killed |
| Sgt. | A | Campbell | | C | Plt.Off. | F.C. | Sutton | C |
| Flt.Lt. | E.W. | Campbell-Colquhoun | | | Fg.Off. | K.R. | Sutton | |
| Plt.Off. | S. | Carlin | | C Killed | Plt.Off. | S.R. | Thomas | |
| Fg.Off. | W.F. | Carnaby | | Killed | Sgt. | E.R. | Thorn | Killed |
| Sgt. | V.R. | Chapman | | C | Sgt. | J.R. | Toombs | C |
| Plt.Off. | M.C. | Corner | | C Died | Flt.Lt. | A.J. | Trumble | |
| Sgt. | W.E. | Cox | | C Killed | Sgt. | R.C. | Turner | C Killed * |
| Sgt. | V.W.J. | Crook | | C | Sgt. | | Wake | C |
| Plt.Off. | | Debree | | C | Plt.Off. | T.D. | Welsh | |
| Plt.Off. | C.C. | Ellery | | C | Plt.Off. | D. | Whitney | Killed * |
| Sgt. | C.S. | Emeny | | C | Plt.Off. | M.H. | Young | |
| Sgt. | F. | Gash | | C | Sgt. | R.B. | Young | Killed * |
| Plt.Off. | R.S. | Gaskell | | | | | | |
| Sqn.Ldr. | G.D. | Gavin | | | *Killed during the Battle of Britain | | | |
| Plt.Off. | H.I. | Goodall | | Killed * | C - Aircrew | | | |
| Plt.Off. | G.H. | Hackwood | | Killed | | | | |
| Sgt. | O.A. | Hardy | | C | | | | |
| Sgt. | L.H. | Hayden | | C | | | | |
| Plt.Off. | F.D. | Hughes | | | | | | |
| Sqn.Ldr. | P.A. | Hunter | | Killed* | | | | |
| Plt.Off. | C.E. | Johnson | | C Killed * | | | | |
| Plt.Off. | J.T. | Jones | | Killed* | | | | |
| Plt.Off. | D.H.S. | Kay | | Killed | | | | |
| Plt.Off. | P.L. | Kenner | | Killed* | | | | |
| Plt.Off. | F.H. | King | | C Killed* | | | | |
| Plt.Off. | W.R.A. | Knocker | | | | | | |
| Sgt. | A.J. | Lauder | | | | | | |
| Sgt. | P. | Lille | | | | | | |
| Sgt. | W.H. | Machin | | C Killed* | | | | |
| Plt.Off. | M.H. | Maggs | | C | | | | |
| Sgt. | A. | Martin | | C | | | | |
| Sgt. | W. | Maxwell | | C Killed * | | | | |
| Plt.Off. | J.C. | Melvill | | | | | | |
| Flt.Lt. | A. | Montagu-Smith | | | | | | |
| Plt.Off. | W.R. | Moore | | C | | | | |
| Sgt. | W.J. | Murland | | C | | | | |
| Fg.Off. | A. | O'Connell | | C | | | | |
| Fg.Off. | D.H.C. | O'Omalley | | Killed* | | | | |
| Plt.Off. | R.H. | Percy | | Killed | | | | |

| Rank | | No. 85 Squadron | |
|------|---|------|---|
| 1940 | | During the Battle of Britain | |
| Sgt. | G. | Allard | Killed * |
| Sgt. | H.H. | Allgood | Killed |
| Plt.Off. | P.W. | Arbon | |
| Plt.Off. | J.R.A. | Bailey | |
| Sgt. | T.C.E. | Berkley | Killed |
| Plt.Off. | J.L. | Bickerdyke | Killed |
| Sgt. | G.B. | Booth | Killed * |
| Sgt. | T.M. | Calderwood | Killed |
| Fg.Off. | W.F. | Carnaby | Killed |
| Sgt. | A.H. | Deacon | |
| W.Off. | F.H. | de la Boucher | Killed |
| Plt.Off. | C.E. | English | Killed * |
| Sgt. | J.H.M. | Ellis | Killed * |
| Sgt. | W.R. | Evans | |
| W.Off. | F.E. | Fayolle | Killed |
| Sgt. | G. | Goodman | |
| Plt.Off. | A.V. | Gowers | Killed |
| Sgt. | K.W. | Gray | Killed |
| Flt.Lt. | H.R. | Hamilton | Killed * |
| Sgt. | C.E. | Hampshire | |
| Plt.Off. | J.A. | Hemingway | |
| Plt.Off. | H.W. | Hodgson | Killed |
| Sgt. | H.N. | Howes | Killed |
| Sgt. | R.S. | Hutton | Killed |
| Flt.Lt. | J. | Jefferies | Killed |
| Sgt. | L. | Jowitt | Killed * |
| Fg.Off. | R.H.A. | Lee | Killed * |
| Plt.Off. | A.G. | Lewis | |
| Plt.Off. | J. | Lockhart | Killed |
| Plt.Off. | J.E. | Marshall | Killed |
| Sgt. | C.A. | Rust | |
| Plt.Off. | S.P. | Stephenson | |
| Sqn.Ldr. | P.W. | Townsend | |
| Sgt. | F.R. | Walker-Smith | Killed |
| Sgt. | E.R. | Webster | |
| Fg.Off. | P.P. | Woods-Scawen | Killed * |
| Plt.Off. | P.A. | Worrall | Killed |

* Killed during the Battle of Britain

*Opposite and above: The lists of casualties in my first two squadrons. I did two further tours after them, in 125 Squadron and 600 City of London Squadron.*

*Four Battle of Britain pilots years after the war. From left to right: Air Commodore A.C. Deere, Group Captain Peter Townsend, Group Captain Denis Gillam, Air Vice-Marshal Johnny Johnson.*

disliked the company – so together we went to see the Squadron-Commander and volunteered to join a neighbouring squadron who were short of pilots. Ivins peered at both our resignations for some time before commenting: 'It would look funny if I was to volunteer too.' We were not posted.

# Chapter 16

# Chasing German Reconnaissance Aircraft

Genius, I opine, is bred of the marriage of angels to fallen women. The brilliant can be a little wild and the brothers Atcherley proved no exception. The brothers were identical twins. These two, from the same split egg, looked alike and the stories that were circulated about them hardly distinguished one twin from the other.

Group-Captains Batchy and David Atcherley commanded the aerodrome of Fairwood Common in turn, teaching the advantage of combining a first-class intellect with great flying ability. They were big, powerful men; both unmarried and with a trick of doing with little sleep; turning up at the flare-path in the early hours of each morning, chatting to all and sundry as equals, of whatever rank. Formidable in judgment, they were universally loved. Giants; intellectually they moved among men like a farmer among his cattle.

The Atcherley legend related how one of them, dressed up in a scarlet hunting coat and top hat, was accustomed to do the crazy flying at Hendon before the war, sitting outside the cockpit astride the tail of a Moth, regulating the controls with reins. When winter came, one of them used to carve his initials in the snow with his wing-tip, low-flying over the aerodrome. One of them flew through the hangars. One of them had commanded a Hurricane squadron flying off the frozen fjords during the campaign in Norway . . . and so the legend ran on. I remember Batchy Atcherley borrowing our small communications aircraft to visit a friend on an aircraft carrier. I saw his large frame wobbling off the ground in this thing and learnt, a day or so later, that he had landed on the flight deck when the lift was down, fallen down the hole and the captain of his ship had been compelled to raise his burning guest out of the lift shaft with the ship's crane and drop the aircraft over the side. I remember one occasion when Batchy sat with us over a flying supper in the early hours of the morning, and said, pointedly: 'Flying is a young man's game. You chaps are about right, I am too old for it.' Soon after that, he left us to command Kenley and soon after that the following tale was told of him:

One fine Sunday morning, 11 Group were surprised to hear two German fighters claim to shoot down an RAF aircraft into the sea. Following correct procedure, although they had no record of an aircraft in their control room, they sent the crash-boats out, who picked up Batchy, one of their senior station commanders, sitting mid-channel in a pilot-type dinghy, with bullet wounds down his arm. Growing bored of office, he had borrowed a Spitfire from one of the squadrons and flown across occupied France to Paris to beat up his old haunts. The Germans picked him off just before he got back.

To be a success in the Air Force, as might well be guessed, a man required character, and character was to be measured in quantity rather than quality. Hence it followed that to be deficient in some portion of the anatomy raised a man well above the level of his peers, a leg or an eye missing was heaven, to be short of a couple of fingers even was a qualification for a minor Elysium. Had we only possessed a pilot with an excess of limbs, two heads or three legs, I think he would have been elevated to Air Rank almost there and then. This was very much as it should be.

Fighting in Russia and Libya had withdrawn the war from us. The Germans flew through our sector only aircraft directed to shipping and weather reconnaissance. At this period, each afternoon, a Junkers 88 used to round the Scilly Islands and, flying five miles outside the shipping lane, and at sea-level, travel along the north coast of Cornwall and Devon into the Bristol Channel as far as Lundy Island. Then, turning north and west, he would fly parallel to the swept channel that passed along the south coast of Wales into Milford Haven and the Irish Sea.

The weather reconnaissance left Cherbourg peninsula before daylight and flew at varying heights up to Carnsore Point, the south-eastern tip of Ireland, recording temperatures and pressures. Now the shipping reconnaissance flew beyond it, so that it was in fact quite by chance that we came to know of these activities. Sometimes they flew too high and for a few minutes were observed by the CHL radar, sometimes trawlers reported them, or the 'Y' service. This last was a series of wireless stations that used to pick up and record all the wireless messages German aircraft transmitted, and most useful it was too. For, so soon as they talked, we had their position; and ever so often a loquacious wireless operator would make the journey and lo! we had half their track mapped out.

We were fortunate at this time to possess two highly intelligent controllers; the one, Squadron-Leader Shipwright, was a Jew from the film industry; the other Patterson, was a lecturer in anthropology from Trinity College, Cambridge. Between them they worked out a system by means of which, if we could obtain one fix on an enemy aircraft, we could extrapolate from there, and reasonably guess where it would be in ten minutes' time. For Germans are good soldiers, and military men can be guaranteed to repeat their behaviour, however foolish such repetition might be.

In this way we soon drove the shipping reconnaissance out of the Bristol Channel in all except the thickest weather. A section of 87 Squadron flew from a small aerodrome on the Scillies and picked off a couple more of them as they were rounding the point. Three of us were patrolling for another when it spotted us, for we were not flying close enough to the water. It approached too near to the convoy, probably in order to avoid us, and the Spitfires picking it up, machine-gunned it into the sea. Soon afterwards Pat Boyd, an Australian, intelligently directed from the ground, attacked another, which blew up. A fifth was spotted in the afternoon, quite by chance, and quickly destroyed. Thereafter they gave the game up.

The long-range weather reconnaissance was more persistent, much harder to come by and gave us better sport. We consumed large quantities of petrol in these sidelines for small results. But they provided us with training, so that they were useful exercises as well as fun. They were also dangerous. Other night squadrons had taken on long-range day-fighting over the sea for a hobby, had lost a crew or two without result and had then desisted. For we operated up to 150 miles out to sea; and since the aircraft were not fitted with feathering pumps, should one engine be put out, we might well have to swim for it.

Success came from the quality of the pilots. The Newfoundland Squadron never had a good sector, for it was too small a place to be able to put sufficient pressure on the Air Ministry, although we importuned the Newfoundland representative with requests to aid us. A good salmon-fisherman on an indifferent beat cannot gaff much. So it was only when these crews left the squadron for other units that they had their chance, then they distinguished themselves.

James Mathews, a pale, diminutive clerk from the Prudential Insurance Company, was such a one. Known inevitably as Jim Prune, he became a most able pilot. He was much later posted to a squadron escorting the night-bomber force over Germany; and by the end of the war, had picked up at this most difficult game, a dozen German fighters and several decorations. He later became a test pilot for the Fairey Aircraft Company.

His pleasant pal, Johnnie, in whom there was nothing counterfeit, was less successful; for he lavished himself so upon women, he was unable to concentrate upon flying. David Atcherley, the Station-Commander, told him that the only thing that could stay out every night and still fly was a sparrow, but the information did him little good.

Jamie, an attractive young New Zealander, succeeded with everything that was asked of him. He was later posted to a squadron covering the Normandy invasion, and had brought his score to fourteen before being compelled to return to his home country. For both his brothers had been killed in the Air Force, and his father having died, he must cultivate the family acres.

John Turnbull was an independent, pig-headed Canadian, both useful qualities in a fighter-pilot. His face was long and strange. He spoke characteristically of his first kill. 'I was sorry for that bastard' – muttered he – 'but God! I loved it!' I used to go duck-shooting with him and another Canadian pilot, Nobby Hall, whose favourite exclamation was: 'Holy Cow!' Turnbull performed feats of great virtuosity, including a successful night-attack on a power station in Northern France, which from the photographs we all held to be inaccessible. He then joined 600 Squadron in North Africa, bringing his score up to double figures before being sent home for a rest.

Pat Boyd was a reticent Australian pilot, a combination of qualities which was unusual. He was a thin, self-possessed figure and a most able pilot. Later he was posted to the Far East, and picked up a DFC or two fighting the Japanese.

Together we worked up suitable tactics for this long-range interception, and over the Atlantic and the North Sea the squadron destroyed in all six German aircraft, and damaged or probably destroyed nine others without loss to ourselves from enemy action. This was a small reward for the labour we put in; but I am convinced that the squadron was much better for this mastery of day-fighting, when the time came to return to its proper role of fighting by night.

And for myself, all this year, I worked continuously on a new system of night-defence. It was controlled by a Master-Fighter a year or two before Bomber Command ran the attack with a

Master-Bomber. It developed the highly successful technique which Stevens had used in 1940. For it co-ordinated the search-lights, fighters and flak into one unified system and proposed to use the radar-equipped fighter force, which was the only effective killer, to the full. By conventional methods, the defence never used in one raid more than 30 per cent of their available aircraft. In addition to the standard defences, we stacked the target areas with night-fighters. As all enemy bombers had perforce to come to us, it made their destruction simpler and quicker than chasing them around the sky.

It was difficult at twenty-two to sell a new design for the defences of England to senior officers. I found myself, at one point, very lamely and uncertainly addressing a meeting, under the chairmanship of Air Vice-Marshal Orlebar of Schneider Trophy fame, composed among others of one general and three brigadiers, all twice my age. It taught me that to invent a new technique is easier than to sell it and the same type of mind is unlikely to manage both. Anyway, the design was wholly correct although it was allowed to modify our defences by only a fraction.

We had our misfortunes too. One night a message came through from Operations saying: 'We're unable to contact Q for Queenie and the Observer Corps say they think an aircraft has gone into the sea off the Smalls. It may be someone else, of course, but we ought to try a search. The crashboats will be going out any minute now. What can you do about it?'

We replied: 'Two or three of us will load up with flares and as soon as the ships are in position, light the sea for them.'

'Okay,' replied the controller.

So we set to work collecting additional flares and in a quarter of an hour were airborne. We had met these accidents before, and knew that if Queenie did not call up on the wireless shortly, or come in to land with a bent wireless set, he was a dead man.

The moon had just set, high cloud hid the stars. A cold front was approaching from the west, so as we flew into it, the amount of cloud increased and the base of it descended.

I checked. Temperatures okay, pressures okay.

Poor old Queenie! Poor bloody navigator! It is sufficient to cut one's own throat as a pilot, but to have it done for you as a passenger – poor sap!

Control came through on the wireless, 'Fuzzbuzz calling. You are over the right place now, can you see the ships?' I peered through the darkness which was too wholeheartedly black to allow of distinguishing land from water. There were two or three little lights below.

'I think so. Thanks very much. Hallo Ran, are you in position yet?'

'How the hell should I know! Yes, I can see you to starboard. In position, now.'

Ken let go two flares. One failed. The second glowed like an aspiring sun.

I saw three ships below as if it were day. The light was reflected from the ceiling of cloud which was lowering upon us. Even from up here you could see that the wind had risen and the waters were in turmoil. The flare spanked a wave and went out. It was again pitch dark, St Dunstan.

'Did you see anything, Ran?'

'Not a sausage.'

'Here goes the next.'

Ken, on whom conjurors have nothing, released a third flare through the hatch. For two minutes there was light. We search, then all is solid darkness once more. Thus we sent down eleven flares.

Thanks to the Observer Corps, we knew for this once the exact place where the aircraft was seen to hit the sea. The ships are in the correct position. The sea is rough and bitterly cold. Speed is therefore essential if someone is to escape. But who could escape, I wondered. Whoever does on these occasions?

'Hallo Fuzzbuzz, send out our relief with more flares.'

'Fuzzbuzz answering. No, I think you had better come in and land, we have some more information for you.'

We turned our backs on Queenie, who might, I imagined, have been sitting, distraught and chilled, in a small yellow dinghy riding that fearful sea, certain in such weather to die before daylight.

We flew back, feeling our way through the dark night, wondering the while if more could have been done. Ran and I landed, parked our two aircraft and together entered the dispersal hut. The electric light was bright in our eyes. Gordon rose as we came in. It was he who had been practising with Queenie.

'I had you chaps recalled,' he told us, 'because I saw most of the accident. Old Queenie caught sight of me – there was still a bit of moon – and thought he would take evasive action. He did so in no mean way. I should think he put the stick hard over for he turned on his side and went straight down. I actually saw a flash a second later, but thought no more of it at the time.'

'It was black as a nigger's arsehole below cloud,' Ran put in.

'Yes, what probably happened was that his gyro toppled and he was too slow going onto his turn and bank instrument, once he had dived.'

'I suppose his navigator may have baled out.'

'I very much doubt it.'

# Chapter 17

# Fairwood Common: Attacking a Reconnaissance Ju 88

So the days passed; and we, while living comfortably, became more expert at our profession. Over the same period, the boffins were improving the quality of our radar, so that we were soon able to dog-fight to the limits of the aircraft's manoeuvrability, although, in fact, we never saw the other aircraft except on the screen.

During this period I went on a short Rolls-Royce course to Crewe; also, on a Flying Instructor's course at the Central Flying School and a fortnight's blind-flying course. These helped to give me a sound theoretical background.

About this time, a tall, young Newfoundland pilot joined the squadron, by name Jack Reid. He was nearly deported for some early errors and I interceded for him. His voice was so loud and hearty, he was reputed not to need his wireless, for, it was hazarded, he need only open his cockpit window and shout. Before he left Newfoundland he taught in Sunday School. His father saw him off to the war. 'Remember, son,' he said, 'never smoke and never drink.'

'He was carrying my suitcase for me at the time,' Jack laughingly added, 'and it had two bottles of whisky in it.' He survived a year, before ramming his target while practising attacks at night and dying that way.

I was learning a little how to see by night and by day, and the results were surprising. For instance, a properly camouflaged aircraft, flying by day hard down on the sea, was invisible from a mile or two away. But if you were the lower, another aircraft would then be silhouetted against the sky and thus become apparent at six or seven miles. It had once seemed to me to be difficult to come at an aircraft out of the sun, as the protagonists in the previous war had claimed, for the sun is so small. But I soon discovered that it fills a quarter of the sky at twenty thousand feet, for at ground level the glare is lessened by the atmosphere. Again, a properly camouflaged aircraft becomes quickly invisible against the blue of the sky. But if you are higher than your opponent and can set him off against the cloud, he will stand out at seven to ten miles.

The night sky is deceptive. At dusk and dawn, and in the north at midsummer, we found it helpful to work our prey so that it should stand against the glow, either of the first or of the last light; or of the perpetual glimmer that in June obtains high up over England during the whole course of the night. The moon casts a path across the sea; in it you can see a convoy from fifteen to twenty miles. With a full moon, if there is no cloud, you cannot see a twin-engined aircraft beyond six hundred yards; but with a full moon playing on a sheet of cloud, you can spot an aircraft against it from a mile away.

Pat Boyd and I took off on a patrol one morning, which did something to vary our otherwise unaggressive existence. It was still dark when we left the ground, but control had informed us that the Germans had switched on their wireless beacon at Cherbourg; this usually denoted that the Weather Recce would fly that morning. For once, events went almost as planned. There was heavy cloud over base, but eighty miles south of Ireland, we found only a layer up to five thousand feet. It was broad daylight when we arrived. We were flying at about fifteen thousand feet in an area which we had computed was the most likely to be crossed. In due time, ground control picked up an enemy aircraft a hundred miles to the south, coming north. They lost contact. However, we were vectored to the area where he was conceived to be, if he had maintained both his usual course and the normal economical cruising speed of a Junkers 88. And there, in fact, he was, far below us, indeed ten thousand feet below the height suggested from the ground.

I was surprised. I had so often searched within a maze of cloud for German aircraft that were not there, to actually sight one below us, a lonely black dot, astonished me. We moved into the sun and slid down it. The enemy pilot was flying just above the cloud-tops, so that he could plunge into them at a moment's notice. I did not wish to risk losing him, and so descended upon him as fast as I could, Pat keeping close beside me on one flank. The soft cloud passed beneath us. It dazzled in the sunlight, a sheet of ice, polar, stretching floe upon floe to the furthest horizon. On a Hurricane, the bullet-proof windscreen was kept warm by the air from the engine in front of it. On a twin-engined fighter, such as a Beaufighter, the plate-glass gradually took on the temperature of the air about it. And since it is a massive sheet of glass, it remains cold while you dive into warmer air, and the warm air condenses on it. My windscreen was misting in this way, so that as we dived I was agitatedly rubbing it with my leather glove in the hope of being able to see something through it. Our prey grew larger, and we caught sight of the details and the German crosses on it as we approached. Partly because I could not properly see and partly because I was impetuous, I turned out of the sun and in behind him a moment too soon. He still did not notice us; but fearing that he might escape us if he did – for if his gunners had been keeping a proper watch he must have observed us at once – I opened fire as we closed in on him, starting with a long burst from about five hundred yards. As we closed fast, two shells exploded on the fuselage by the rear gun-position. At this, he turned slightly port, dived into cloud and was gone.

He gained France. We could not follow him with our radar sets, since the cloud was too low for the early make of radar we carried to be effective. But the 'Y' service picked up a transmission, in which he reported that he had been attacked by

British fighters who had overshot him. He was also plotted in several places on his route home.

After following him for a while, as it transpired, fruitlessly, we again turned north. And eventually ground control directed us to land in Anglesey, because the weather had closed down over the west of England. So we flew north and put in at the aerodrome called Valley.

Soon it was high summer. 'Me Greasy' was the nickname of a sturdy pilot of some seriousness. He, Jamie and I were sun-bathing and shared the beach with the sand-fleas.

I flew a kite, asking: 'Me Greasy, tell me, what will there be to do in Civvy Street as disinterested and as worthwhile as this job of ours?'

Jamie butted in: 'Me Greasy just reads the *New Statesman*, he does not think in those terms at all. Feeding the poor, Me Greasy, isn't that right?'

'I see what you are asking Jim, even if you do ready the *Daily Telegraph*,' Me Greasy replied thoughtfully. 'Let me propose, getting married, perhaps, and rearing children.'

'That is the sort of answer tapeworms make,' Jamie said.

'I suppose New Zealanders do not marry,' Me Greasy ob-structed, 'they just rub noses.'

'Marriage is not so admirable,' Jamie argued, 'it is a method of dying in comfort.' 'Well, how do you answer you own question?' Jamie then asked, turning to me. In parenthesis he added: 'New Zealanders never answer questions. There are no questions in New Zealand. We plan things. That is why the country is so dull.'

'I don't know the answers,' I admitted. 'I believe there will be people after the war, perhaps Me Greasy here, too, if he can avoid the Reaper, who will find a humdrum, respectable peace-time existence lousier than our life now. Take Prune and Johnnie and Pat and Randall. What on earth will they do?'

'I know what Johnnie will do,' Jamie said, 'the local girls will be lifting their skirts whether they want to or not.'

Me Greasy said: 'There isn't a substitute, Jim, really there isn't. I'm scared half the time. I would really like to get back to school-mastering in Northumberland. But I would not have missed this for anything. I have made friends, rotters like you and Jamie and Torchie. We would never have come together in the ordinary course of things. And you, Jim, would have been rich and not talked to us. Jamie would have been biting the tails off sheep or that other bit they take, not so, Jamie?'

'We are extra, specially, extremely, good people in New Zealand,' Jamie said, 'that is why I do not much wish to go home. I would like to get to Oxford, like Jim here.'

'In peace-time, the substitute must be Plato's vision of the good,' I said sententiously, having just been reading.

'In a hundred years' time,' Jamie said, 'I do not suppose it will make two hoots of difference what we have done or thought or said, or what our opinion of the good used to be.'

'But it makes a difference to us now, surely, for us this moment matters.' I answered.

Me Greasy replied to me: 'Let me tell you I would not have missed flying fighters for anything. I dreamt of this life as a kid. It is all I ever dreamt of.'

We were lying in the sand, the Bristol Channel quiet and calm in front of us, the Gower summer, Port Eynon and young limbs becoming sunburnt. Within a year, Me Greasy had been shot down by our own ack-ack, while defending the Algerian harbour of Oran, and killed.

# Chapter 18

# The Shetland Islands and Peterhead

The shipping reconnaissance had left the Bristol Channel, and the weather reconnaissance had been driven by our long campaign as far west as the Old Head of Kinsale. It was now beyond our ken.

But to the north of Britain, the Germans reconnoitered freely. The first reconnaissance took off before dawn from Holland, I think from Gilze-Rijen, and flying up the North Sea, parallel to the east coast of Scotland and a hundred or more miles out, finished his milk-run by landing at Stavanger, in Norway. This recorded the weather. At the same time a Junkers 88 left Stavanger, crossed the northern point of the Shetland Islands, and then proceeding south-west, reconnoitered the Atlantic shipping lanes, reporting the position of the American convoys. It was a long, dangerous trip over that waste of water, and we came to esteem the men who made it.

Heretofore, they had gone unmolested. For they were too far from land for the Spitfires to operate, and the Beaufighter squadrons in those parts had either tried the game and given it up, or been forbidden to attempt it. So in the winter they switched us on to it, and we sent a detachment north, which flew either from Sumburgh in the Shetland Islands or from the most easterly aerodrome in Scotland, Peterhead.

Ivins, our Squadron-Commander, had been posted away and given command of an intruder squadron, attacking German aerodromes in France, at which activity he was shortly afterwards killed. His successor, Paddy Green, was a large, pale broker who had been a bobsleigh champion in his Cambridge days. He was an excellent pilot and a first-class administrator, accustomed, so it seemed to me, to soften up his seniors by presenting them with pheasants which I had shot.

Anyway, he got us the job; and sent off the less experienced pilots to try their hands. They gained their experience; but, as was inevitable, made the initial blunders, so that as a result of bad tactics or inaccurate shooting they damaged one or two German aircraft, alarmed the rest, but really achieved very little in what was then virgin territory.

Desmond Hughes and Johnny Turnbull then went north, and being most capable, soon put one or two German aircraft into the sea. Returning from leave, I joined them on the Shetland Islands, and thus made my first acquaintance with those northern waters. It was now mid-winter.

The trouble with England, a Yankee pilot had once observed, is that you keep running out of land. When flying, we largely lived out over the ocean and had grown accustomed to the winter water, which when we skimmed low over it, showed itself as green breakers of ice-water, the waves piling one upon the other, as alien as they were a million years ago, before man stalked the earth.

It was pointed out to us that Air Marshal Tedder came from Lerwick, the capital of the Shetlands; that the inhabitants were of Danish descent, and that the winds were so strong across the islands no tree would grow upon them. We could believe all of this. Activity came only at dawn. But our enemy, now thoroughly alarmed, was passing seventy miles north of Herma Ness, the most northerly point of the Shetlands, and at that range flying under the radar screen.

The main runway was short enough. You landed just over the top of the waves onto tarmac which led straight into the sea again, so that you could afford neither to fall short of it nor to overshoot it. The wind was blowing half a gale when I took off on my first patrol, which both permitted us and compelled us to use the runway that was shorter still, a groove carved through the rocks, resembling a railway cutting.

We took off at dawn. Climbing up into the day we passed the seaplane base, and soon began to see the outline of the islets in the grey-green light. They were an afterthought of land in the sea, little changed since the longboats ran up their sounds. Then, as we proceeded north, the rocks passed beyond sight. It had been freezing at ground level; where I was flying it was minus thirty degrees. Clouds in lonely isolation passed, sighing their soft sighs and underneath them a scurry of snow, the flakes falling and disappearing on the waves as rapidly as human bodies.

The sea was a light-green gravitational field, waiting to draw an aircraft in and engulf it. I thought of the race I had seen passing the Orkneys and raging through the Pentland Firth.

I had earlier wondered whether, skimming low over the breast of the water, if I had been lost, I could have gauged the approach to land by the birds. Whether, if I had changed skuas for guillemots, or the larger petrels for Mother Carey's chickens, I could say that I approached land. I studied it, but it did not seem practical. But I came to admire the fowl that lived in the lap of the water, not only passing just above the waves, but flying down into the troughs, just lifting a moment when a wave creamed over, then down again into the smoothed depression.

Nothing came of our patrol. The enemy passed undetected to the north, and returned, four hours later, slipping cunningly between Fair Isle and the Orkneys in a flurry of snow. He was too wise for us. So we went south again to Peterhead.

A week previously we had been in luck. The petrol dump at Sumburgh was filled direct from the ships. The tankers were accustomed to back up the petrol with sea-water to push the last of it through the pipes. A careless operator had debauched the aerodrome store, after its proper load of 100-octane fuel, with a large portion of the North Sea; which sank, according to the laws of specific gravity, to the bottom of the reservoirs. A week earlier the level of petrol had dropped, and all our bowers had been fouled. Hudsons, working on anti-submarine patrol, disappeared into the ocean; our squadron was luckier, for the fault was discovered before anyone was drowned.

But so it came about that on a certain morning we had only one aircraft serviceable, and its gun-sight was set to one side of the bullet-proof glass, all points against us for this type of work. However, Ken Dear and I slipped into it and we were away, alone, before daylight.

Day broke over the water; and with it came news that there was a German aircraft in the sector south of us, coming north. We were flying in a gap in the stratus. Below us was a sheet of white cloud, above us, another uninterrupted layer; between, it lacked the misty winter light of those skies but was crystal clear.

'Turn port, China one-eight, on to one-zero-zero. The bandit is forty miles south-east of you. I think he is about angels fifteen.'

'China one-eight, China one-eight, we've lost him. Orbit, orbit, he should be near you now.'

Then we saw him. We saw a speck in the sky at the limit of vision, serenely flying north.

I opened up to full throttle, climbed into the cloud above us and began to stalk him. I was forced to reappear once or twice to check his position, but he did not notice us. We had to be close to him before he saw us, for if he was given the smallest grace he could dive away into cloud and would be lost for ever. In fact, we were lucky, for we broke cloud a thousand yards from him; we were well above him, and could dive straight onto his tail as he passed from starboard to port beneath us. It was a Junkers 88. He saw us at once and dived, releasing streams of tracer which passed us in abundance, above and below. I held my fire, and concentrated on closing the range.

A theorist who is a pilot hazards his own head. And following the immortal Dr Johnson, I must admit that such a risk makes for concentration. I was tenacious, not of a kill but of proof of a theory. Certainly, the only person to be nearly killed demonstrating that this type of interception was possible and reasonably safe, was myself on this occasion.

For our prey now made a mortal error. I opened fire and struck him on the tip of the port wing, planting crocuses of light there. I imagine that our true airspeed was between four and five hundred, and had he continued his dive, spiralling for cloud, he must have escaped. Instead, on being hit, he changed his mind; and began a long climbing turn to port. We were now between two and three hundred yards apart; his aim was improving, mine remained weak. I saw bright flashes from the muzzle of his guns. I hit him several times on the port wing and engine, firing at him in small bursts, that nearly always registered, but never with more than one or two strikes. I had him full of lead, however, by the time that his gunner, who had unhappily survived all this, placed me in the centre of the pattern. There was a monstrous roar, a strange stink, and my starboard engine misfired. I broke away. I last saw the slender shape of this aircraft, I can recall it clearly, flying down towards the sea, in which, as we later discovered, it crashed. For during the rest of the day, German rescue aircraft concentrated on that lonely piece of ocean.

I remember quickly taking stock of my position. I cut the petrol on the starboard engine, which was failing, and switched off. A bullet had come in through the perspex, passed through the flap of my right ear, blowing the earphones out of my helmet. I thus heard the full roar of the motors, louder for the hole in the canopy. Another bullet had punctured the tank holding the de-icing fluid, which spilled about the cockpit, giving rise to the smell. Another had penetrated the instrument panel and passed my waist. Later, I found there were two bullets in the port engine, one in the starboard, three in the nose of the machine, one through the starboard mainplane and others elsewhere.

Our combat had taken place almost half-way between Scotland and Norway. We had thus much flying before reaching land; but the good engine was holding.

I feared to go into the sea. At Sumburgh, I had dipped my hand into a transparent rock-pool and the cold had terrified me. It is not death which strikes home, but dying. I was sorry for my enemy because I was sorry for myself, and embraced all who might sink through these aching waters in a general prayer. Reasonably, I am a little sceptical; but I cannot forego my earliest training; so that in great joy or terror, I supplicate. We did everything we could to help ourselves, and then, laughing at myself for doing so, I fell back upon magic. For in mid-winter the northern seas are terrible.

Control sent off two Spitfires to accompany us as we struggled back on one engine, which took us almost an hour. They were very welcome. I imagined to myself afterwards how some old pilot, in his latter days, perhaps delirious before death, might call from the depths of his fever: Bring out the Spitfires! Bring out the Spitfires! – so already had perished Waterloo.

After a night in hospital I went away on ten days' leave.

# Chapter 19

# The Death Of Gordon

I had been pondering the notion of 'importance'. It had seemed to me that for many people, life in wartime took on a significance it had previously lacked; the end was given. And it was these distinct, sharp, unquestioned values which were the greatest gift of War to the indecisive. Purpose is a notion that has been as yet scantily studied.

All animals have it; for attitudes have histories and prehistories. A zebra, irritated by a tick, will forget it for a lion. With men, the idea of importance has been elaborated; we are universally conscious of it, but rarely self-conscious about it. Necessities are food, drink, shelter, a mate. But once Prometheus's bare back is covered, he enters on a period of greater artifice.

Our life acquires a soft silk cocoon of important events, protecting it from natural and significant winds. I must pass my examinations; I must buy a new dress; I must meet John at five. And so we move from a tea-party and a place in a team to questions of precedence at dinner. Importance gives impetus to our existence, direction to our personality. And by this soft white covering we shield ourselves from the greater questions.

This system is by man made. It enriches our life and gives a gloss to the skin of the young, who without keenness might themselves be lustreless. In the young it is as flexible as their soft muscle; in the old it stiffens; they fasten not upon something gracious but fill the board-rooms of power.

To resemble another above all is to have emotions in common.

If a friend is moved where I am unmoved, shocked where I am complacent, at ease when my bowels are wrung, agreement about politics goes for nothing. For it is in the placing of importance where lives differ; and we may soon construct on the sandtable another's existence once we can map his emphasis.

Originality lies there, and a proper grasp of unreality and of music is revealed in this. There are no separate civilisations. Before Magellan, the great neolithic travellers introduced societies to each other. I cannot, say, compare this or this, for the Great Tradition runs through them all. We must break out consciously for the first time, and utter personalities that have never yet been seen. I would proclaim the age of the Uncommon Man with his new 'Very'.

This much I was working on when Gordon Denbigh, my flight commander, came to me one morning to say that we were not allowed to follow the reconnaissance aircraft into the sector south of us. The Air Officer in charge of that Group had refused to let his own Beaufighters try this game, and it would appear, our seniors told us, as if, were we to go there, we were showing him how to clean his own washing. And since the German reconnaissance pilots now avoided our sector, there was not much that we might do. Yet it had been recently impressed on us, in a special order sternly read out to us, that the times required that we should take every opportunity to destroy the enemy.

So we put our heads together and planned something different. The plan was mine, the decision to put it into operation was Gordon's. It was quite simple. Fighter Command had never operated over Norway, so an aggressive gesture would come as a surprise. The idea was to choose a day with cloud, and to cruise along the coast opposite Stavanger and the other aerodromes on which Messerschmitts were based. Day pilots are confused by cloud. We intended to be intercepted by the Me 109s. One of us would fly just under cloud as a decoy, the other would climb up into cloud and wait for the two day-fighters to appear on his radar screen; then while they were chasing the decoy, he could dive out of cloud onto their tails. It was a simple trick, and one the Germans used on us later – but now we were to be thwarted by bad luck.

'Provided we keep a good look-out,' I said, 'and turn back at once if the cloud is unsuitable, I think there is very little risk.'

So after breakfast on a Sunday morning, at about 10 o'clock, we took off. I talked Gordon into being the decoy. Flying a wide line-abreast formation, we travelled east. I see by my log-book, it was December 10th, 1942.

The meteorological officer had been a little vague about the weather over Norway; he had reported it covered in cloud, but he had not said what kind of cloud it was. There was a warm front approaching Peterhead from the west, one of those great rain-filled barriers that drive in from the Atlantic to be shattered by the mountain ranges of Europe. They bear in front of them a shield of cloud that begins with cirrus at thirty thousand feet and in sharp declivities lowers its echelons to ground level in the centre of the storm. We climbed up under this shield. As we went east, the base of the cloud rose and the cloud thinned. We were up at twenty thousand feet, and even the cirrus above our heads was sketchy. We could see Denmark, dark in the distance. Where Norway should have been there was a bank of cloud right down on the mountains, in which it would not have been safe to fly; but twenty miles short of the mountains our own cloud tailed off, leaving us in brilliant sunshine.

'No good,' said Gordon.

'Agreed,' I replied.

'We had better turn back,' said Gordon.

Then came disaster. We were aloft in the cold, winter sunlight, the temperature was far below freezing point, the sea green and immense beneath us. I saw a long, long roll of white smoke pour out from one of Gordon's motors and unfurl into an ominous banner behind him. We were at our greatest distance from Scotland, having that moment turned about. Gordon could have taken a chance and parachuted over Norway; instead, he headed out to sea, expecting to be able to fly upon one engine, even though the Air Ministry had failed to supply us with the pumps needed for feathering the propeller.

Bad luck! We were of necessity taking chances. Judging by our flying record, the odds against that sort of engine failure in the half-hour when we were furthest from land, must have been a thousand to one. But against those odds it happened.

'Have you jettisoned petrol?'

'Yes.'

I dropped with him. We flew seventy miles or so before he sank to a few thousand feet. His Beaufighter was steady and sleek beside me, with one propeller spinning. I wondered whether he had fired off his ammunition; and if he had changed from high to low ratio on the supercharger to accord with our decreased height. I asked him a few questions. I wanted to check further, but did not wish to panic him and so kept silent.

As it became painfully evident that Gordon would finish in the sea, I left him and climbed to fifteen thousand feet so as to be able to speak on the wireless to our base. They could send a ship for him or the Catalina flying-boat, which specialised in picking aircrew up out of the water. So I left him and in climbing through cloud, lost sight of him. Soon Peterhead were able faintly to answer me, with a feeble voice, barely audible. I called for help and asked them to fix my position, so that they would know rightly where he was. They most annoyingly fumbled this once or twice but at last fixed me correctly.

'Gordon, are you all right?'

'No, Jim, I am going into the sea.'

That was all.

I went down to search for him.

From aloft, you may detect patterns in the sea, observe the change of colour where a river enters or where the coastal waters drop off a shelf into the deeper ocean. I had watched many ships burn. But I had never encountered so terrifying an ocean. The storm had been following us out over the water. We were returning into it. A gale had caught the seas, normally wild enough at this time of year, and moved them to their depths. To notice a dinghy from the air, you must fly almost at sea level. I flew above the waves, and thus raced past not the huge interminable ocean, but each individual comber, hissing, spewing, rising up onto the back of its neighbour, striking at the air before dropping with a crash onto its belly, dissolved into a deep, swept trough of profound foam. The lonely waters were white, laced with greens; bottle-green, grey-green, pale-green, ice-green. It was not possible that a man could survive in this welter. We were in mid-ocean, half-way between the two lands, a grey, leaden sky above us, and all around, pawing up at us, this arctic waste in terrible confusion.

There was nothing. There was not even an oil-slick to be seen. When I had only petrol enough to return to base, I left. The destroyer that set off to search for Gordon put back again to harbour. I could not land at Peterhead because of the storm, but returned to a Coastal Command aerodrome further north, landing nervously and distraught. It was another two days before the destroyer and the search aircraft could go out there, though, as we all knew, it was hopeless by then.

# Chapter 20

# Fowling

We returned to Fairwood Common. I was given Gordon's job. Life proceeded as before.

I had come to know the sea-marshes during the course of the previous winter and something of the habits of the local wigeon. Two Canadians, the pertinacious Turnbull and Hall, a plump, agreeable pilot, joined me in this. We worked the evening and morning flights, for during the day the birds roosted on the sandbanks out to sea, and the marsh was but a forlorn waste of mud, pocked with shell-craters on the range. Ribs of wreckage protruded from the sands.

The village of Llangwydian was set beside it, whose villagers pastured their cattle on the wigeon-grass. Occasionally the beasts stuck fast in the mud of the creeks, or were cut off by the spring tides that were hastened in by the wind, but usually they cropped safely enough beyond the sea-wall. The men kept a shotgun and did a little fowling of an evening. I began to yearn with a deep yearning for their sane existence, the secure cottage life with its seasonal routines, the warm kitchen grate and the children playing beside it.

When I could, I hung to the marshes. For although I had almost reasoned myself out of blood sports, I loved this waste, and I am by nature a hunter. So, too, my mind was occupied and diverted from its more pressing considerations.

The expert fighter-pilot, I am convinced, is the man who has turned over in his brain every eventuality, so that when emergencies arise, he will instantly do right; even as the greatest wits labour for their spontaneous observations. Failure comes from the divided daydream. It is even more true of wartime pilots than of manufacturing plant; they fatigue while waiting. So I was happy to take my Clumber bitch, and there forget yesterday and tomorrow, and those imaginings on which I pined.

Though often close to cities, as are the marshes that edge the sea-roads to London, these wastes disputed by the tide are still about the wildest places upon earth. The African bush is not wild by comparison. Sea and sky meet in pathetic gloom. It seemed to me then, among knot and sanderling, that men discover in nature quite largely what they put into her. The deceit of poets is the selective eye. For to them, nature is not ravening; but is a lone curlew, the linnet, the vine-leaf by the Moselle; the woodcock silent in the moist leaves; the feathered feet of doves.

The desires of animals are but the earlier heat of the sun, in this way given form and direction. They answer to the sun, as the child owns to its mother. The sun rules by giving and taking away of itself; we are but one animal among many. Nothing it seems is discrete. The gull tearing a crippled bird, the lamprey delving into a fish, the crow that prods out the eye of an ewe, they have their part in us and we in them. The first man of whom we know anything was cannibal.

There is a conspiracy to hide from ourselves the forces of nature that live their separate lives inside us. I refer not now to the angers and the lusts; but to the unspoken impulses that sometimes glow within like lamps. It will be they that overturn the steel and concrete no earthquake moves. When Donne preached, he failed to observe the animal in his sermon.

For we are but parts fractured from the whole. The trapped stoat is haste, the hunting stoat purpose. The lion and the spider consuming their mates do no more than their Creator; thus the seal and the tapered salmon, the blowfly and the wounded antelope. We ourselves are as subject to this fate as was Actaeon, slain among the rustling bushes by his own hounds. We would admire the wing of the mallard, and gloat upon the pheasant's copper chest; esteem the rindfrost; or the gannets' snowfall around Ailsa Craig; but we forget the fox and the bacillus. Tonight, how many leopards purr around, how many kills? These, too, are part of us.

Such thoughts as these developed, while I lay among the creeks, waiting for the wigeon to pass along the big dyke to the open sea. I found it only possible to come by wigeon if, confronted by wild weather, their nerve cracked before my own. Then they would face the dripping gale, beating up into the teeth of it, quibbling, flying low over the ground like starlings. They would not move until the tide could be heard running. A moment ago the gulley was dry; now a splash, barely audible, and you knew that in the darkness the murmuring sea was returning, filling dykes with its sibilants, dykes which had been safely waded an hour before.

One morning I stayed late. It was early in February. Spring sometimes interposes a day towards the end of winter. The wigeon had outwitted us; but the morning was too warm and mild to hasten away, so I walked as far along the main creek as I was able, before lying down on an old gas cape, near to the waves. While I lay there, prone in the warmth, the sort of day on which the first bees come to the marsh, a pair of pintail flighted down the tide. I made a long shot to drop the cock into the water. Juno, the Clumber spaniel, went after him.

The tip of his wing was broken. He splashed along the surface of the water, which ran shallow above the brindled sand. As the bitch approached, he dived. I called her off, for a winged duck will better any dog, and stood ready to shoot again when he rose. He came up; and now the bitch was gone, he appeared unafraid, floating on the stream that was draining to the sea. It was slack tide. The outgoing water was stayed by the waves just beyond us.

I was held by his beauty. His drake plumage was newly

minted, a chocolate brown over the head, the speculum green, wings powdered with white, the chest pale, and one sensed that underneath its sheen, down feathers grew dense and soft. He rode the stream past me, bright in the sunlight, as if I were not there.

The bone never knits. He would never fly again, for I had sniped too straight. My gun echoed across the wide marsh as I stopped him. I was enough ashamed of myself for the incident to stay cleft in the memory; though why I, one of the ephemeridae, should be so nice when Nature destroys all she has created, I am not certain how to justify. But I have used a shotgun little since then.

# Chapter 21

# The North African Convoy

One afternoon, the two Canadians, John Turnbull and Nobby Hall, set out with me to test aircraft which would be used at readiness that night. Taking off, we crossed the coast near the Mumbles, climbing up through a substantial thickness of cloud into the afternoon sunshine. In this way you quit a drab winter for spring.

While we were testing the aircraft, Nobby Hall mentioned over the radio that an engine was giving trouble. He turned back for the aerodrome; John and I flew formation on him, encouraging him. He was losing height all the while, the one prop ominously spinning and like this we entered cloud. He lost height rapidly in cloud. Coming out of the bottom of it, we found ourselves in the grey-bronze winter, the Bristol Channel around us, the dark coasts of Wales just visible to starboard. He continued to lose height but the aerodrome was not far off and I felt that there was a good chance he could make it.

He did not make it.

I have always been at a loss to know whether I should not have talked more to my companion in distress. But when you are fighting panic, fighting a disabled aircraft, fighting weather, for an intruder to butt in with unwanted advice is to make things worse and, for my money, to make panic surer.

We encouraged him the best we were able but his fighter slowly sank and he force-landed in the water. It was once more a tumultuous sea. Where he pitched, he stayed; there seemed to be no skid. Only a great plume of spray fountained into the air, with bits of broken aircraft in it, caping him entirely. We watched. As the spume fell again, it revealed the airframe lying on the surface. There was no movement in the cockpit. It rested there a full thirty seconds, a whale, then it sounded. A merchant ship intelligently altered course to search and, of course, the crash-boats went out, but every wave was surf. Anyway, we had observed it all: no one had escaped.

Then Sergeant Finn went in near the Smalls. This was about our sixth crew to be killed in this way. I think he panicked when his engine failed. Panic is the great destroyer; for often it needs more courage to live than to die. With this news I went away and wept; I felt I had had enough. Thereafter I found that I had reached that degree of sadness which could no longer touch me; the delicate instruments which recorded this emotion were now wrecked; henceforward, when some other mishap would occur I would feel more hollow or more bitter. Death came down the telephones.

The dead usually left behind them parents, or a wife or girl friend to be consoled. The Commanding Officer sent official condolences, friends unofficial. I call to mind the sort of woman involved; instance the wife at West Malling who had been a Ziegfeld Folly. She was some two foot taller than her husband, and when they danced on guest nights, invisible to her tiny mate below, she cast the most ravishing glances at the young pilots whom they passed. Or the 'Egyptian Queen', a swarthy driver at Colerne, who kept a roster of paramours upon her cuff; she would show them to you, officers and men listed together, higgledy-piggledy. Or the Norwegian pilot at Colerne, a handsome fellow of good family, who on his leave married a whore. When he tried to leave her, she hunted him from aerodrome to aerodrome demanding to see her husband; until his commanding officers in despair, posted him to the Middle East. So it went on. Terry, another pilot, recounted one morning, with descriptions of each individual humour, how he had spent the previous night with the female contortionist from the Manchester Variety Show; while Baldy, a middle-aged gunner, leaving the same show with two girls, spent the night in a hearse which had been drawn up by chance in a backyard. It was a broad experience – only the concealed moments were delicate.

'Jim, you will take a flight to Predannock,' Paddy Green now maintained, 'and join up with the Coastal Command Beaufighters to do a series of sweeps through the Bay of Biscay.'

'Thank you,' I replied dubiously; for by now we had lost confidence in our slieve-valve engines. Six of us flew down to Predannock, beat up the aerodrome in great style, and then landed on this pleasant Cornish Station which lay by the sea.

I was tired, not physically but nervously; like a car that runs upon the generator when the plates of the batteries are broken. It runs evenly enough, until something special is required of it, then there are no reserves. Great men in every edition exhorted us to defend civilisation; and in its supposed defence we had worn ourselves. I was thus led to ask what it was.

For I was concerned with the fact that there were two civilisations at work within any society – although so ubiquitous is the division it as yet goes unrecognised – that of children and of adults – the first lyrical, the second commercial. The two are separate, divided absolutely, their eyes rarely meet. In fact so great is this cleavage that historians, who for obvious reasons are adult, have failed thus far to recognise the existence of a once flourishing culture.

Be sure that the child's civilisation differs from that of its parents. Though using the same words she speaks another language, she has other heroines, her cares are different and the objects of her love. Her world is smaller, but it is still the real world, it pounds. The sky is bluer and close, like a ceiling. Her values are different from those of her parents. She has more vowels and fewer consonants. Though she also cheats, honesty and frankness yet come naturally. O, that I were still able to place my hand as frankly in the hand of a stranger!

As yet, for we remain all ignorance, different civilisations clash. It seems that men have not yet discovered in these differences the charm of life and of travel, unaware that differences should be increased and not eroded. Hence, since the Renaissance and the Age of Faith, many of whose virtues were childlike, we see a gradual encroachment upon the once-flourishing civilisation of children, as on all other civilisations, by those great organs of commerce; governmental education, discriminatory legislation, social pressure. The herdboys and the barefooted girls have departed Europe.

It is pre-eminently upon distant islands, and then somewhat artificially, that the Balinese and other cultures have survived. The scattered remnants of the children's culture remain among Europeans, though driven into the deserts, the slums of the great cities.

The paperboys are the herdboys of yesterday. The children of the rich, largely deprived of their own culture and language, the half-educated savage, enjoy neither the music of the child nor the dignity of the adult; but survive, constrained intermediaries between the two.

I do not regret imperialism; I ask only that the happiest civilisation should succeed by its example. There are virtues proper to manhood as to children. But I ask that the lyrical should reach over into maturity; and that the long preparation for dying that takes place in the commercial houses and the Victorian clubs, be lit by some music, some joy, and some generosity; gentle recollections of the happier culture of youth.

We took off, six Beaufighters, the following afternoon; turned at the Scillies, taking a last bearing on St Mary's Lighthouse, and then flew south. We dropped down to sea-level. The aerodrome on the Brest Peninsula was reported by intelligence to contain a squadron of Me 109s and a squadron of Focke-Wulf 190s. We had no wish to meet them, and so flew under their radar net, low above the water.

The Germans were using Ju 88s in wedges of six or eight

aircraft to do their own sweeps far into the Bay of Biscay. They were not well flown, it seemed, and were often crewed by men still under training. Their fighters were more manoeuvrable than our own; but we could climb and dive faster at this low level, and I, for one, expected we should give a good account of ourselves if there was fighting. As we flew past the Scilly Islands they looked already gay with spring. Men in cockleshells fished among the rocks. Oh, how I envied their safety and happiness! We thundered overhead, making for the open sea.

Although there is no cover at sea-level, it had been possible in the Bay for one squadron to jump another, by the simple device of approaching out of the sun; not so often out of the sun perhaps as out of the sun's trail across the water, for on a long patrol the glare becomes unbearable. Air-gunners blink and yawn in the bright sunlight, and although they search, they omit to study that dazzling quadrant of the sky. Perhaps they have been out over these waters during many months, without ever seeing any other aircraft, so they relax their vigilance, and suddenly the enemy are among them, and they have lost every advantage. We fought like pterodactyls above a waste of water.

It was wise to fly as hard down upon the sea as possible. A salt rime collected on the windscreen. We flew in a loose line-abreast formation; convenient enough in attack, suitable for a defensive circle if attacked. There was a little haze to begin with, so that I began to wonder if the smoke of Manchester infected Spain. Later, the weather cleared into a brilliant, sunlit afternoon. And we were as far out to sea as a liner.

One grows close to one's aircraft, attentive to every sound of the engine. I had come to love the massively built Beaufighter cockpit, the lay-out of the panels, the wheels that opened and closed the petrol cocks, the view through the strutted canopy. By then it was my home. Everything in it had been studied, for love of life had prompted me to this knowledge. It was a powerful, clumsy brute of an aeroplane, but, used rightly, a destroyer. Scissors cut paper, paper wraps stone, stone blunts scissors. So long as we avoided single-engined fighters, with our tremendous firepower, we were formidable indeed.

At latitude 46° we turned back. We met nothing. But owing to error in my compass we passed within thirty miles of the Brest Peninsula and the German fighter stations. Flying over springtime Cornwall once more, I would not have changed place with their fishermen for anything. Afterwards, Prune said he was flying so low his speedometer registered in knots.

Next day we made another wide sweep towards Spain. We met nothing. We returned happily to Wales, only then to discover that we had been protecting the great Armada, sailing far out of sight of us, to make the first landing in North Africa.

They told me that I must take a rest. Would you care for a job on an American squadron? Fine, I replied. So for three incongruous months I was attached to 615 Squadron, the United States Army Air Corps, joining them, appropriately enough, on April 1st, 1943. Jim Prune and his navigator, Ken Dear and myself, were liaison officers responsible for teaching and helping to turn out what was, I believe, Uncle Sam's first night-fighter squadron. Needless to say, it was a failure.

# Chapter 22

# 615 Squadron: America's Air Force

'They look like a bunch of Italian prisoners,' I could not help but observe to Captain Ambrose N. Banks, the huge operations officer of 615 Squadron. His enlisted men were arriving at Ayr after crossing the Atlantic in the Queen Mary. Americans, it seems, fade, if parted for a few days from their PX. In years Ambrose Banks was forty, in outlook ten, a delightful character with sufficient humour to be unnettled at this offence. I was to see much of him. He had been a Pan-American pilot in private life, with eleven thousand flying hours to his credit. It fell to me to give this grandfather of flying a demonstration of a Beaufighter, so I stood him up in the back without straps and rolled him round the sky to prevent any misunderstanding between us. After that we were friends. If he were not flying, he consumed each evening a bottle of Bourbon whisky and a WAAF. It was nothing for Ken Dear or myself to be woken in the early hours of the morning, the electric light blazing, and to see a vast, rubicund face an inch or two in front of one's own, requesting:

'Would you care for a slice of roast beef?'

His father, Ambrose said, was eighty and still alive. He used to be hopping mad, Ambrose said, when son returned home, looked his old father up and down and asked:

'Why don't you hurry up and die, you old buzzard?'

Ken had been both a bank clerk before the war and a regular contributor to *Punch*.

Shortly after their arrival, some of the ground crews, a sturdy crowd, assembled in the locker-room. We were to make their acquaintance. 'How did you come over?' Prune asked them. Before any could reply, the cultivated voice of Ken Dear, commenting upon their thirst, made itself heard: 'Dehydrated.'

We were too light with them. I had been sitting drinking beer with their intelligence officers. Someone had observed: 'I cannot see why you people have two intelligence officers. We have one and we can never find anything for him to do.' And then later: 'The only thing our intelligence officers have in common is that they have no intelligence.' This stung.

One of their number nurtured his grievance against us until dark. As I remember him, he was under six foot, but broad and bull-necked with a slab of a face. He was named Fritz. He and Ambrose Banks had been drinking together. In the early hours of the morning they came into my bedroom in the Nissen hut, out of a seeming good-fellowship, woke me up with great clatter, switched on the lights and said good morning to the dog. Ambrose Banks then passed out upon his own bed in a drunken coma. As he left, the blinds were drawn down on his companion's face. The Bruiser went bad. I fear and loathe a malicious inebriate. He threatened:

'I was wrestling and boxing champion in thirteen states.'

I pulled up the white linen and shivered.

'My father was German and my mother Irish, but I am a good American. You would not understand that.'

I thought to myself many things but replied: 'Of course I understand.'

'I won the Golden Gloves contest!' I shivered again, and drew the sheets up further. His voice had been increasing until it rang through the hut. I heard a whispering outside the door. Ambrose Banks was unconscious, Prune was the size of a Jenny wren and could not affect a fight either way; Ken, excellent navigator though he was, was peaceable – a cockney, a disciple of Dryden and Johnson, a humorist, but no street-fighter.

As the fever was reaching a crisis, Ken in his pyjamas looked round the door. He put his hand to the side of his mouth and said in a stage whisper: 'Prune says he is going to smack you in the puss.' The Bruiser blenched:

'No man is going to smack me in the puss.'

Ken retired, and Fritz's wrath descended upon me, re-enthused. The door creaked open again. Prune's blond head appeared. He put a hand to the side of his tiny mouth and said in a hoarse whisper: 'Ken said he is going to smack you in the puss.'

'No one is going to smack me in the puss,' the Bruiser yelled his words. Then Prune disappeared and the cravens left me to my fate.

Dawn was breaking and the first larks had begun their carillon – for summer had moved in on us – before I had talked him to bed. Next night, I took him fly-fishing on the river Ayr – here was an otter working the pool below us – and thereafter we were friends. That meant, however, that he came to see me when he had letters from his mother, usually at an hour that was far past midnight. The letters used to be in verse on microfilm; all about her curly-headed boy. 'Me,' he cried, the tears streaming down his cheeks, 'her curly-headed boy!' He judged himself to be a failure because he had been snagged as a pilot. Of course he was no failure – probably the psychologists had got at him.

Ken trained the radar-operators; Prune and I held the pilots in the way they should go. In fact, while they were in our charge, they did not even scratch the paint off an aircraft. Individually, they numbered among them some of the pleasantest and most generous people you could wish; but as a squadron, they were soft and undisciplined. One cannot easily overrate the contribution of the American Flying Fortresses to actually sapping the strength of the German fighter command, originally at great cost; but not only were Americans unused to flying by night, they seemed as a nation to be lost, if their work were to be personal and lonely.

The Station-Commander came up to me. 'I judge you to be unemployed,' he said.

'I am heavily engaged with my Americans,' I retorted.

'Anyway,' he said, 'next week is Wings for Victory Week in the West of Scotland. I must supply one officer for it. The adjutant will give you a list of your duties.'

'H'mm,' I replied, and went to see the Station-Adjutant. Duties –

(1) Take the Wings for Victory Parade at Kilmarnock.

(2) Address cinemas in Ayr, Troon and Kilmarnock.

(3) Compere a demonstration in the Kilmarnock pool given by 615 Squadron, USAAC. Subject: 'How an airman saves himself by means of his dinghy.'

# Chapter 23

# Wings for Victory Week in the West of Scotland

Ayrshire, Robert Burns country, backed the war. Fisherman and miner, tomato-grower, farmer, housewife, all were supporting it by one means or a second. I was under orders to advise them to save their money, invest it in War Bonds and Buy a Spitfire! Privately, I thought they should be told that for every pound they lent, they would receive back less than ten shillings.

Addressing cinema audiences was thus not over-difficult. I timed my speech to endure three minutes. I fancy the style must have been a shade Churchillian; the phrase 'engines of war' I well remember coming into it. Anyway Prune said it was Churchillian.

The Station-Commander authorised me a staff car for the parade at Kilmarnock. I found, as I stepped out, that the train bands were already drawn up on the football field. Quite shortly I was in front of the microphone to give them my three minutes fiscal enthusiasm. For this I was thanked during ten minutes by the Mayor. The head of the Fire Brigade came to the microphone and for fifteen minutes thanked the Mayor for thanking me. Then the brass was blown, the drums were beaten and the march began.

We nobs took time off to drink tea in the schoolroom. I was left a little out of it for the city fathers were discussing regimental details among themselves. The man with the watch said it was time and we walked with him to the saluting base. They said that I was to take the salute. The base was, I suspected, a beer

130

case placed on the pavement beside the curb. It seemed to be a moot point when you actually got on to your base. No one seemed to know.

Half the city was parading, the other half was watching the parade. The column had wound its way round the town, so as to ensure that every gifted citizen with eyes should see it. The band became louder, it was coming up the street, it was fifty yards away. How does one take a salute? Should one keep one's hand to the cap as each platoon passes, from the eyes left to the eyes front? Or does one simply return the salute and then bring the hand to the side? I did not know. But it seemed to me, as I hopelessly fell back on memories of Gaumont-British, that to restore the hand at once would, if it were wrong, look merely blasé – while to keep the hand at the cap, if it were wrong, would suggest to everyone that I was unaccustomed to authority.

'Eyes left!' I had to decide – further vacillation was impossible. I was blasé.

First marched the Home Guard. Then stepped the Fire Brigade, the Air-Raid Wardens, St John Ambulance Brigade – all this was straightforward. Next came the Boy Scouts, the Church Lads' Brigade, the Boys' Brigade, the Girl Guides, the Brownies, the Wolf Cubs. Each had a kind of salute. Last marched the Women's Institute. They just grinned at me, kind, motherly people. What must one do? I grinned back at them.

Kilmarnock Swimming Pool was the scene of our final drive against the West of Scotland. It is a large, modern pool, surrounded by tiers of seats for the spectators. After this, I thought, we shall have brought ruin to the shopkeepers. Lieutenant John Horne, of Doe Run, California, was to give the demonstration. He did not bother to practise. First, the Commandos threw a bridge across the pool; then came an exhibition match of water-polo; then the Army did something or another, and then Lieutenant John Horne. I moved expectantly to the microphone.

Someone switched on the waves. Lieutenant Horne, dressed in flying suit, with a yellow, American-type Mae West, and a parachute harness to which it was attached, climbed up to the top-board, hand over hand. All eyes were fastened on him. He walked to the end of the top-board.

'Ladies and Gentlemen,' I announced. 'This is Lieutenant John Horne of Doe Run, California.' He bowed low from the waist. The crowd clapped him appreciatively. John Horne was a large, pleasant body, with the pasty complexion of the over-fed.

'He will now demonstrate to you how an American airman saves himself by means of his dinghy.'

John Horne gripped his nose firmly with one hand and jumped sedately into space. He descended quite slowly but the splash was amazing.

'He is now opening the $CO_2$ bottle to inflate the Mae West. This will sustain him while he releases the dinghy.'

I could see him struggling with something. A wave passed over his head. Another wave passed above his head. I played for time, while the city councillors behind me began rather audibly to whisper.

'There is no hurry. It usually takes the Air-Sea-Rescue Service several days to find us.' Lieutenant Horne had turned very pale. He was now spending more time under the water than above. Things were going palpably wrong. The truth struck all of us at once, he was drowning. Someone ran to turn off the waves, and in the ensuing silence, a waterlogged airman splashed to the side and held on to it for dear life, looking much like a rabbit that has fallen into a ditch.

Some days after, a bizarre accident took place on the aerodrome. Midmorning, an enlisted man ran up, shouting that there had been a crash. Three or four of us piled into a jeep and drove at speed round the perimeter track. On the far side of the aerodrome was found a crashed Beaufighter belonging to the neighbouring R A F squadron. We were told the pilot had swung upon take off. He had flown right through the brick-built armoury building, leaving it a mound of rubble, and he had lodged just beyond it. The plane had not immediately caught fire and when we arrived, the dazed pilot and navigator, their arms around the necks of friends, were being helped away. There was a crowd of fifty or more RAF types huddled together at a safe distance from the plane. With a sob the Beaufighter ignited and its six hundred gallons of fuel, its oil-tank, its twelve hundred rounds of explosive or incendiary cannon ammunition, its eight thousand rounds of machine-gun ammunition and its oxygen ammunition that had been stored in the armoury began to explode too. I saw the Flight-Commander in charge of the gunnery training unit, Pete Ottwell, a Flight-Lieutenant whose face had once been burnt but which had been restored to him, and at the time looked nearly, but not quite, human, gazing at the flames. What he was experiencing ran through me. Then a voice piped up from the crowd – 'There is a third man in there, there is a third man in there.' No one knew, no one moved.

A minute later, in the middle of the furnace, a face appeared in the navigator's window: Shadrach, Meshack and Abednego. There had been a passenger in the plane who was concussed and the heat had aroused him. Two of us ran to assist, but he was quite capable of helping himself. He clambered out through the navigator's escape hatch and we helped him away. He proved not to be much injured. We went back to watching the fire.

Could it be? The wheels had broken away from the fuselage and lay on top of the rubble. In the middle of the explosions a wheel tipped very slightly and then again. Three or four of us ran over and found the armament-sergeant buried in the rubble, topped by a hefty Beaufighter wheel. The heat had brought him to and his first stirring had been nudging the wheel. He stayed a substantial period in hospital but recovered, I heard, not much the worse for it.

It was the only fire of that sort I ever saw which was funny.

# Chapter 24

# Journey to Gibraltar

Time came for our generous Americans to depart. I flew to
Portreath after them in an Oxford trainer. They were briefed;
they objected to the guides provided for them to lead them to
Gibraltar; and then they were ready. Ken Dear and I bade each
a sad farewell, impressing Stevenson's maxim upon him as we
pumped his hand: To travel hopefully is better than to arrive.

After that I was sent as an instructor to Charter Hall, an
operational training station in Scotland, where a pleasant lady
with an 18th-century country house on the Tweed entertained
some of us, and so relieved the tedium of that existence. Thence
to Honiley, where we started a new operational training school
for night-fighter pilots. For a time, I ran a school for teaching
instructors. The Station-Commander had been number two in
charge of the Hurricane wing in Russia and told an interesting
tale of that adventure.

His principal point was, that to drink vodka against the
Russians it is necessary to copy them and line your stomach
with large quantities of fat. He added that the best looking of
the younger pilots were much in demand by the Russian pilots
as dancing partners and that the RAF were held in high esteem
by the Russian bomber-crews, the senior Russian officers, apparently, actively objecting when the RAF wing was sent back
again to England.

I selected myself the two most interesting pupils on the course,
a Maori and an Australian railway porter. The porter handled

his aircraft like a trunk. The Maori, Riwai by name, had good hands and flew admirably. But soon after he joined a squadron, I heard later, an engine of his aircraft cut after take-off. He followed the book, landed straight ahead – for it was night – hit a tree – crashed and died.

Thence, at the end of my period of rest, I was posted to one of the early combined-operations courses held at Largs, in the West of Scotland. It gave a preview of the Normandy invasion, instructing the officers of all services who would be landing. Most of those attending were responsible army and naval officers, the Air Force being represented by a Military Police Officer and myself; both of us specialists in a form of warfare quite unconnected with the matter in hand. Whenever the Air Force were asked for their advice upon a point, the Military Policeman always recommened: 'I should bring up the heavy bombers and flatten it.' By the end of a long fortnight on landing-barges, field-telephones, rocket-craft, supporting tanks, etc, which had begun to drag beyond belief, a young naval officer who had been sitting beside me, came up and said: 'I felt as bored as you looked.'

I rather think Ken Dear had decided, after our experiences over the sea, that I was not long for this world. Furthermore his wife was reluctant to let him go abroad. I desired, for my part, to do my next tour away from England; to do as much travelling as I was able at His Majesty's expense. So I teamed with a burly Canadian, Ross by name, who had been fox-farming before the war. He sported a big, amber moustache and a ruddy, hard-drinking face, above the wide expanse of his basic industries.

We had volunteered to go to Italy. Ross took a shortened, almost a correspondence, course on navigation; we carved our way through formalities and in a trice were down at Portreath ready to leave the next morning for Gibraltar. I felt a free and easy man again. With us, also waiting to leave, was a young New Zealand pilot, Emery, who had been an air-gunner with us in 264 Squadron in the old days. But now the few who had survived from the early period of the war and had remained with operational squadrons, could tell a tale or two of their experiences, some of them most moving. Emery was such a person. When radar came in, he had converted from being an air-gunner into a radar-operator. He told me that when he rejoined a squadron, they crewed him with a pilot whose nerve had broken. One night they spun a Beaufighter from sixteen thousand feet. Emery said that he tried to bale out but he was trapped and flung around inside the belly of the aircraft as it rotated to the ground. At two thousand feet the aircraft came out of the spin of its own accord. The next night his pilot spun again, rotating into the ground on his last turn in before landing. The pilot was killed; Emery luckily recovered after a long period in hospital.

At daybreak, with a false dawn, we flew off for Gibraltar. As before, we took a last navigational fix on Scilly, gave a wide margin to the fighter stations on the Brest Peninsula, and headed south across the Bay. We flew at our economical cruising height, about eight thousand feet, with broken cloud below us. They had given us only forty rounds for each cannon, but I was in the saddle again, and with just enough ammunition to make an attack worthwhile. Above cloud it was cold and clear.

We were fortunate. Many pilots completed a tour in Coastal Command without seeing a U-boat. We crossed to Gibraltar but once, searching predatorially for something to attack, and behold! A conning tower and a long, white wake in the sea. I spotted it for a moment, quite clearly, through a gap in the cloud below us. We had been advised not to attack a submarine, should we see one, but the briefing was chiefly intended for the inexperienced ferry pilots taking aircraft out to the Mediterranean War. It struck me, that, however long I lived, should I live, I should never again have such a chance, so I slipped into the sun and came down pat onto it.

At this time U-boats were lying on the surface shooting it out with the attacking aircraft. Ross suddenly sighted the submarine and, confused on account of its size, shouted: 'He's got a flakship with him.' I dared not hesitate. As I dived onto it, I had to decide whether this was a destroyer or a submarine, for it was a vessel with a big displacement, and I had to decide whether it was ours or theirs. I concluded that it was a submarine; and I knew that the odds would then be twenty or thirty to one that it was German. So we swooped.

I trusted that the sound of its own engines would deafen the watch. The slender hull was boring eastward through the water, the green combers washing over it and draining off. We were north of Spain; at that low altitude I saw nothing but an unending, heaving seascape. There was one man on the conning tower. I centred the hull of the ship in my sights and fired. In the turmoil of water, anxious as I was to identify the boat as ours or theirs, I did not notice where the shells struck. I raced over the figure on the conning tower; his hands were still in his pockets.

Then Ross said (because he flashed at random his identification light): 'He is flashing the letter of the day, the Allied recognition signal.' So I climbed up again to continue with my travels. I cursed myself, figuratively gnawing at my knuckles for endeavouring to sink the British Navy. Down the coast of Spain and Portugal we travelled, the little fishing villages white in the increasing sunlight, the bare, brown mountain ranges climbing up behind.

We reported the incident to the intelligence officer upon landing at the Rock. It was, he said, indeed a U-boat. And, so he assured us next morning. Coastal Command sank it after receiving our fix on its position. For my part I kept quiet, following that sage maxim: no names and no pack drill.

A little earlier Italy had dropped out of the war. It seemed to me then that Germany would be wise to sue for peace. The possibility of the conflict being soon over had both pleased and alarmed me. I yearned for peace and a return to sanity. But at the same time I had turned all my thoughts round this extraordinary profession; for four arduous years I had studied it day and night; and indeed as a group we had developed it from its original crude and rudimentary techniques into an art, requiring of all of us loving degrees of skill. The artist loves his art. Overridingly I wanted peace; but I was also reluctant to become a pianist without a piano or a painter without that canvas which he himself had helped to create.

# Chapter 25

# From Gibraltar to Italy

After England and frostbitten November, Gibraltar was gay with sunlight and full of wine. The airmen serving there were still tanned, and wore short trousers and their summer kit. I found the sunlight dazzling.

There fell on that day the ceremony of presenting the key of the fortress to the Governor. The broad, white-walled square was lined with garrison troops, who were watching it. Away from England, the soldier's scarlet ceremonial took clarion meaning. The bugle summons the living and the dead.

We were given a rest before leaving for Rabat, in Morocco. That night Murray Ross and I went round the cafés, dining variously off wine, steak and bananas.

Next day, drowsily in the sunshine, I wondered by what strange trick of Fate we had come here. We were pinched, it seemed, where there was intellectual error, at that point where Nietzsche, Marx and Cantuar quarrelled. Throughout history there has been a compact between the soldier and the scholar. For the scholar, with his ideas, serves to weaken the resolution of the enemy, or to charm him, or if the enemy be captive, to pass him into a willing slave, a Turk's janissary. The soldier seduces the scholar, whose class-room propositions thus gain the cogency of bayonets; so that the ordinary man, so dilute his brain, confounds inference with high explosive. The scholar arms the attacking infantry; he convinces him of his valour; he promises him Progress or Paradise; and advances before him with a Cross, a Geiger Counter or a Crescent.

The fiend, taking Him up to the top of the hill, promised Him all the kingdoms of the world. Such a deal the Crusaders made, and the Saracens. Hegel took bribes. The Russians had requisitioned, after Marx, his Estate. Had Comte been more serviceable to their Revolution, he would have been Religion and that other Heresy.

How few arguments are considered, even by the greatest intellects, separate from their lay arm! Then too, politicians are deluded by historians, who wish to sell their books to earn money and fame. Politicians depend upon historians for assignation with their tombs. Readers enjoy stories about crime, romance and famous men. Nothing in Hollywood has equalled the build-up of that brilliant thug, Napoleon. Thus historians provide for their readers the appeals both of the *Tatler* and of Peter Cheyney.

Politicians are men. They have been taught over the centuries to suspect the values of the priest. Being men, they will not think for themselves. So they accept without question the values of the historian.

Again, politicians are men. Despairing of celestial abundance, they hope to be raised from their mortality at last by the touch of the historian. There is no such thing, said the great Hollywood magnate, as bad publicity. So they either reproduce the actions famed in their history books, as did Hitler; or they just act; that they may gain their perpetuity along with the Children in the Tower. The scholars praise the successful, for it is the aristocrats who are royalists. But the mind is a correcting gyroscope; we cannot go on thus.

That day we flew with three other Beaufighters to Rabat; thence to Maison Blanche, the airport for Algiers. Here we delivered our aircraft. We stayed a few days at the transit camp, Fort de l'Eau; but as Stevenson, who was one of the original pilots in 264 Squadron now commanded the nearest Beaufighter squadron, I left the transit camp to stay with him at Regghaia aerodrome. I soon borrowed his aircraft. But we did not lodge with him long enough to do more than two or three patrols along the Algerian coastline, time enough to tell everyone how to trap their local reconnaissance aircraft but not time enough to prove it. So we left, I suspected, with some reputation for boastfulness. Stevenson was shot down and killed soon after.

Both town and countryside were congenial. By night, the scent of Africa wafted to us, the dry grass smell. Laurie Dixon, Desmond Hughes's red-haired navigator, was passing through on his way back to England. We lunched together off Algerian wine and this was his downfall. Trouble started when we sat at a pavement table. For the Arab urchins gathered round him, crying: 'Gingerrrr! Gingerrrr!' He grew incensed; to such a pitch was he roused that he caught the offenders and bent them over his knee while I walloped them with a rolled-up paper. This was fair. But he was by now grown so passionate from wine and goading, that he caught the venerable burnoused Arabs as they passed down the street, bending the ancients around his knee, expecting me to strike them too. Instead, I did my best to apologise. They took it in happy part.

Later, we passed through Tunis, and were carried by the Americans to Montecorvino, the fighter station near Salerno Bay. 600 Squadron was stationed there. Here I met again Johnny Turnbull, Desmond Hughes, Paddy Green and an old Czech acquaintance, Joe. Having completed a most successful tour of operations, all were waiting to leave Italy. Their tents were laid out pleasantly in an orange grove, half-way between the mountains and the sea.

# Chapter 26

# Private Warfare

Winter in Algeria had resembled the Cape of Good Hope winter, cold and wet. The rain struck through the canvas of the tents, or blew in through the chinks, so that blankets and battledress were always moist. When we reached Italy the weather around Naples was mild, but with the New Year, the snow piled up against the mountains. Then the night winds became keen.

Once the landing at Salerno had been secured, the German Air Force lost interest in the Italian Front, so that I arrived on December 3rd to a squadron that had little to do. I occasionally picked up an Italian 16-bore shotgun and wandered the fields in search of snipe. I used a young cowherd to drive the birds for me, arranging the drives with the aid of a pocket dictionary. This sufficed. Yet I could never persuade him to distinguish snipe from the ordinary small birds of the hedgerow, so that he would spend an hour rounding a flock of starlings.

A colonel had lectured the combined operations course at Largs on the correct packing of landing-barges. He cited, as an example of how not to do it, an instance from Salerno. The infantry who landed in the first wave were pinned down onto the beaches and apparently for several days it was touch and go whether they would not be thrown back into the sea. 'Imagine our horror,' he said, 'when from the second wave of landing-barges to sail in, one hour after zero hour, there should emerge with an Air Force Officer, a piano, a double-bass, a number of smaller stringed instruments and a complete set of brass!' The offender was the officer in charge of the advance party for 600 Squadron. He was, he told me, also in charge of the band; and unless he had taken his instruments with him, they would surely have been forgotten.

Anyway, I organised a concert with them at Christmas to be my contribution to the common weal. This was a mistake. The Welsh tenor refused to sing unless someone brought him the music for 'Your Tiny Hand is Frozen'. A Flight-Sergeant was not to be allowed to tell his dirty stories, I was instructed – they were too filthy. Also it was insufferable that a certain Warrant Officer should, for the fourth time, recall 'The Death of Dan McGrew'. Then the rain leaked through the marquee in which the instruments were housed so that the ivories of the looted piano came unglued. This was but the beginning. Fortunately I was then detached to another aerodrome; for when Christmas Eve arrived and with it the opening night, the cast were so drunk, the show had to be cancelled.

I came to love Italy. I found the south priest-ridden and the resulting poverty extreme. But Catholicism also seemed to lend itself to poetry and music; so that the poorer peasantry were in many respects happier than the wealthier people of the stern, Calvinistic north. I did not care to eat, when there were starving children beyond the wire who watched each morsel forked into my mouth. Yet I ate and threw to them the remains.

I had met Jamie, the best of my friends from 125 Squadron, shortly before leaving England. Together we had worked out how raids into Northern Italy and across Yugoslavia to the Danube could be undertaken from Foggia; so after Christmas, as the moon waxed again, I arranged the trip into the Po Valley. For I was quite certain that it was an area ideally suited to night interdiction, and since the Germans did not move transport by day, a proper hammering of these areas two and three hundred miles in their rear by night, might well bear fruit. Since this was an exploratory trip, I planned to travel north up the Adriatic, cross the coast near Rimini, and come back among the ravines of the Appenines. I borrowed a navigator, Telford by name, since Ross was sick and must return to England. We practised together.

It struck me, from what I remembered of my trigonometry, that if we dived at an angle of thirty degrees the range of our target would be always twice our height. The Po Valley is very flat and the altimeter could estimate our height accurately enough. I planned to attack vehicles from the front, so that their forward speed should compensate for the drop in the cannon shell if we opened fire at six or seven hundred yards; while if I fired a little short of them, the shells might ricochet off the road into the radiators or the windscreens. If you survived in the RAF, and had so gained experience, you were allowed to wage your own war much as you pleased.

We left Salerno and flew east to Foggia, refuelling there. It was full moon. We took off in the early morning for it seemed to us that the defences might at that time be asleep. We crossed the coast at Termoli. We flew low above the Adriatic, which reflected with occasional crystal, the moonlight. There were fishing boats around, using flares to attract the fish, and to begin with we wondered what these lights might be. South of Ravenna we turned in, opened up to full throttle and dashed across the coast. No one shot at us.

You could always detect the position of the front line. On our side, because we held command of the air, the roads were lit by the glaring headlights of diesel trucks that groaned, bumper to bumper, in a long line from the rearward bases to the front. On the German side, all lights were masked. Then again the Americans always shot at us; while the Germans, whom I imagine preferred to save their ammunition, rarely did. So we were happy to operate over their side of the line.

But so far back as Bologna, the German trucks were also lit; they rolled along the roads beneath us, as in peace-time, unsuspecting. We came down upon a set of bright headlights. I switched over to fire and pressed the button. No sooner had we fired than the lorry was a furnace. I was appalled. By its own flames Telford saw it crash into a ditch. We fired at two or three more lorries but without noticeable result, for unless they were tankers, they were unlikely to reveal the damage we had done. Then Telford spotted a train.

A shadow was moving along the Bologna-Reggio line which I discovered to my alarm was electrified; for a steam train readily reveals itself in moonlight by the trail of white smoke. And I had been depending upon this. Then the train stopped at a station. Someone, probably the guard, was holding a light, and I lined up my dive onto that one small glimmer. As the shells struck, the target was illuminated by their explosions. A signal box was in the line of fire, which seemed to shake like a Felix fort in one of the old films. Exploding shells ran along the train. I climbed up into the darkness. Twice a brilliant glow lit the sky; as if there had been a carbon arc-light warming up. I thought then, that it was perhaps ammunition burning but incline now to believe that the train fused. We attacked another lorry or two, then, when our time was up, turned south again.

We rode among the mountain-peaks in full moonlight. They were mantled in snow, from the base to their seven-thousand-foot summits. Cirrus flecked the bright sky. I stayed below the level of the mountain tops to avoid radar detection. The moonlight played upon the wings, bright, almost as if it were day; above and below us all gleamed a ghostly white. So we travelled up the valleys, passing the blanched mountain villages and the medieval cities of Italy; leaving Florence, Siena and Rome well on our starboard side; but passing near to Perugia and Lake Trasimeno. We crossed the line at Cassino; neither army shot at us. Then down past Naples to Salerno, as the green and mauve light of the morning vied with the moon before passing into the pink gills of day.

# Chapter 27

# The Anzio Beach-Head: February
1944

Towards the end of January the professionals began again to fight their war. They landed a large force south of Rome, and General Patton being absent, failed to achieve anything further. For many months we guarded them. My American squadron, 615, operated from the same aerodrome and in the same sector as ourselves but were ineffective. So we were compelled to concentrate on our proper role, night-fighting over the German side of the line. For this reason, I never got to the Danube.

Ross had injured his spine wrestling in the mess and returned to England. I cast around for another navigator and found – Willie. Willie was not for this world. He was inchoate and not really able to distinguish between Wesleyans and Lesbians. He dwelt on some mystical plane in which the rural England of Blake and Cobbett existed. He babbled of green fields. He was also airsick. His wife wrote poetry. One of his best friends was a Neapolitan pimp called Joe, a honeycomb of sensuousness, who offered Willie his wife for a night as a mark of friendship. I forget whether Willie accepted.

When Paddy Green left 600 Squadron – he left after the landing at Anzio had been secured – he bequeathed us the best groundcrew and the worst aircrew it was my fortune to work with. Happy was one of the senior pilots, not very successful at his work but a superlative character with whom to spend an unlikely evening. He was the sort of man who would have drawn his Bible from a circulating library. He was tall, middle-aged, with a tense, furrowed face. His accent was of Lancashire. He was called Happy, I supposed, because he was by far the most miserable man in the squadron. But sugared up, his spirits soared.

In the company of these two friends I came to know Italy. After the landing at Anzio, I lacked the time to explore further. But for the mid-winter lull Willie had been given a stolen jeep by an American friend. So we kept it as our private vehicle, driving into the historied mountains with it of an evening, acquainting ourselves with the villages. Our favourite retreat was Valle di Maddaloni, a small village as yet unspoiled by the soldiery. When we first entered the café there, the villagers treated us like animals at a zoo, but as the novelty wore off, we became friendly with all of them. We were entertained first of all by the gentry. This family kept a daughter they wished to marry off; a plump, brown, cheerful signorina who played the piano to us. The first night on which we visited them they gave us good wine, the second night moderate wine, the third night *vino di tavola*; for we had not proposed to their plump daughter. Then there was Domenico, a slender, handsome animal, a boy of fourteen who said proudly that he was destined for the church. For in the Naples district was the birthplace of St Thomas Aquinas. We taught his whole family the game of snap; his uncle, feverish for victory, openly cheated. We met, too, the local fascist, a swarthy villain who denied his politics. And some youths, who professed to have bombed the British Navy in the Mediterranean, now showed us photographs of their Savoia Marchetti. We had the last laugh; for soon they received their call-up papers – they showed them to us ruefully – to join those Italian squadrons which were bombing the Germans. As it happened, Roddy Knocker was on the east coast and in charge of the aerodrome from which the Italian squadrons operated.

But it was an evening with Happy which brought me a little trouble, for it was so joyful we overstayed. I wished to see the ruins of Herculaneum and Pompeii, Happy an exhibition from the girls, so he agreed to accompany me if I accompanied him. It proved, of course, to be no exhibition he wanted. In addition, Happy was ambitious to drive a tram. We boarded one; but since we were in Italy, there were already five uniformed drivers. So Happy drove it from the back, while the official drove it from the front. This was not popular, since Happy was applying the brake while the real driver was accelerating, and vice versa. So they took Happy forward to give him the wheel. Since he was so enchantingly content driving it, no one took offence, while for good measure, I mollified them with gifts of cigarettes.

Thence, I do not know how, we entered the apartment of a stranger. There was a very pretty Neapolitan girl there with a Geordie private who was her fiancé. He spoke already a beautiful Italian. By this hour, Happy was beyond noticing the nicer points of deportment and since he had no Italian, he asked the Geordie to translate for him while he made love to her. I sat back and warmed to their comedy.

In the past, the stamina of a horse decided the range of a language. Today your airman, given an unswung compass or a wrong wind, may be a language out in his navigation. To overfly five historic speeches between breakfast and lunch is the European practice. Although there are cosmopolitans, the charm of over the hills rests in distinction and difference. It is this tender uniqueness which a foreign speech protects. The ploughman following behind his horse, his wife at table, the country boy, these are not likely to be bilingual. Ignorance, then, excludes the flavoured joke and the happy retort; you are left at supper with little more of conversation than the smack of eating.

Yet the good soldier is uninhibited by his lack of learning. Abroad, he will more than compensate for his lost home life. Shift him, he has his feet under another table. Indeed, there is grace to the tongue-tied and a favour to the shy; for conversation, especially with the young, is most moving if through the eyes; the more moving, perhaps, for that it is so incomplete.

To the first time there is a charm repetition may not match.

To a strange tongue there is hope men may be speaking wisely and wittily; only with translation comes the knowledge that they speak as banally as the rest. Private and particular speech deprives us of universal communication, yet it has served as a protecting womb for the furnishing of new manners. Perhaps it is in this way, though in small, that two who do not fully understand each other live together more nobly than among the friends who know them at their worst. For they breathe a little mystery, they enjoy a fresh start.

There is a world beyond words that logic may not touch, for subject and object and predicate are inapplicable to it. From this world issue art and poetry. The dramatist, requiring the deeper note, heeds insanity. Lear spoke, whilst the cliffs trembled. The unknown tongue may irk; but to the young, the slight, shy communication of smile and eye, touches all that is required. She who speaks my language requires to know no English; for the common alphabet is ecumenical, beyond dictionaries.

Happy and I were exiled for being absent from camp. But the first ten days of the attack upon Anzio having passed, I returned to the west coast; and soon after, virtually ran, tactically, our forward night defences there, until the line had reached Florence and Leghorn. We lacked a second flight commander. When such a one did arrive eventually, he crashed his aircraft almost immediately and was removed to hospital. Laurie Styles took over command of the squadron from Paddy Green and proved to be the pleasantest of men.

The squadron had earlier lost a plane over Anzio. The Squadron-Commander instructed someone to gather up the effects of the two missing men and pack them off to their next-of-kin. When he came to the navigator's tent, he found that the chap had himself already packed everything neatly and put a farewell letter to his wife on top of the pile. Interestingly enough, the prescient navigator was not killed but made prisoner and so I was able to meet him at the end of the war. 'How did you foresee this accident?' I asked him. 'Oh,' he said simply, 'it was fairly rough over Anzio and I felt it was coming.' That was his inadequate answer.

The battles for Cassino developed underneath us. From our Olympian heights, we saw the massed artillery give a silent fireworks display; the agony on the ground, until translated by the mind, resembled the luminous algae in a wave. I did not doubt that shells, coursing through the night, passed around us, like the dark missile meteors that passage heaven beyond earth's atmosphere. Sometimes the fighting on the beach-head grew desperate; as the German tanks sought to drive the defenders into the sea, tracer would pass across the ground, its full range to us but an inch. The salient of Anzio was not only commanded by German artillery which lobbed shells into the harbour, but important for our purposes, swept by their radar. Ships burnt around the beaches, as in the old days they had flamed around England. Tankers were torpedoed.

When German bombers came in to attack they dropped clouds of tinfoil, called 'window', which confounded the radar. Or they came in singly; and as we turned onto them, they were vectored away from us by their own ground stations. The squadron lost two crews with the same trick which Gordon and I had tried to play. For they sent in a bomber with a night-fighter flying formation on it; and as our crews closed on the pair, which appeared on the tubes but as a single blip, the fighter broke away from the bomber in a steep turn, coming in again behind. Our pilot still concentrated on the aircraft ahead and was shot down before he knew what had happened.

In the middle of one short, chaotic raid on the beach-head, Willie picked up a chance contact. We closed in on it. Etched against the Milky Way, I saw the black shape of a Ju 88, his hooded exhausts tranquilly flickering. I closed in and fired. He exploded. We flew through a galaxy of sparks. Then followed that prolonged pause as the burning wreckage tumbled three miles. Where it finally hit, it bellowed into flame.

# Chapter 28

# Anzio: Spring, 1944

When it came, spring was welcome.

Willie and I drove one pleasant afternoon out to our private village. A mile or two away from it, I dropped off the jeep and told Willie I should meet him at the café. I made my way across the terraced slopes, noting how crocus and daffodil budded earlier here than in England. Cloud, hustled by the wind, was scudding just above my head. A shower of sleet started. I looked for cover, finding a sort of shelter made of turf and logs which resembled a bear-trap. I enjoy squalls, and I felt grateful as I crouched down against the wet, for being alive.

We were on duty again the following night. We patrolled for three hours in the evening but nothing came of it. It seemed likely that there would be a raid after the moon had risen a little before dawn; so I resolved, if another aircraft was called for at that hour, to take off again, myself. I had come to sleep lightly so that I could lie on the truckle bed in the operations lorry and hear all that was said, waking only if the message should be important. Sure enough the raid came. I called for Willie, grabbed my Mae West and hurried to the aircraft. Unfortunately, because I was so far behind with sleep, I had not woken up. Outside it was bright moonlight and freezing. We were flying off an aerodrome that had been newly bulldozed; it was closer to the line than our old one; and so shortened the journey to the beach-head. The Americans who made it had dug a number of pits to serve for a simple drainage system. The earth which they had excavated was piled around the side of the hole. I remember how I solemnly climbed this pile of earth, which I could clearly see (although I was sleep-walking), and fell horizontally into the pit, the bottom of which contained a foot of mud and water. This woke me. When I climbed into the aeroplane, cursing every conceivable portion of Creation, I felt like a rugby player after a long game in the rain. As luck would have it, the first bandit which we were vectored after was a reconnaissance aircraft at twenty-four thousand feet, at which level the temperature was unmentionable. I froze. After that a sharp raid developed. We were put on to another enemy plane, made contact with him, and closed in. I caught sight of his silhouette; it was a Ju 88 travelling north. I closed in behind and a little below, and raised the aircraft's nose to fire. The guns did not fire. I fired again, again nothing happened. Willie checked the guns, I checked the fire and safe mechanism, still without result. We followed him right under the tail, like a dog behind a bitch, the seventy miles to Florence. He never saw us. His large black shadow hung permanently in front of us. Finally, resigned to my fate, I dived away and left him. It transpired that a piece of grit or a drop of water had entered the electrical firing mechanism from my muddy hands. I was very disappointed. To make matters worse, it was broad daylight when I returned, still caked in mud, to the witty amazement of all. Had I been less vexed, I am sure now that I could have persuaded them that we had landed the other side of the line and done a little hand-to-hand fighting.

Towards the end of February, Vesuvius erupted. Pumice destroyed about eighty light bombers stationed on the aerodrome, I think it was Pomigliana; so, for one reason or another the bomber wing took over our aerodrome and we moved to theirs. Just prior to the eruption, Happy had climbed Vesuvius in the company of an ancient guide who confessed to being seventy years old. Vesuvius rises steeply four thousand feet from the plain. When Happy commented upon his prowess, the guide said that formerly he took up two parties a day, but now, he added, if he made the climb twice, he could not satisfy his wife. An unshaven professor of terrestrial physics at the University of Naples was observed measuring the heartbeats of the animal with a sort of stethoscope. A wall of lava reluctantly descended upon a village. The village priest placed a cross before it to arrest its movement, but the lava overwhelmed both cross and village in its passage. Secretly, we rather hoped it would fill in Herculaneum and Pompeii as well, so that they could have the fun of digging them up once more.

I was filled with awe. I perceived how it was that Yahweh had been from the first a volcano-god; and how from this exuberance hagiographies had arisen. Dusk was its best period, for then the ash was lit. It was hurled from the vent several hundred feet above the crest of the mountain and cascaded down in a golden shower; but no sooner had the one jet begun to fall than the next jet belched skyward again; and so played this enormous fountain of fire. Above the mountain a soiled cauliflower of cloud rose through the clear Italian sky to sixteen thousand feet. At each breath, the bottom of the cloud surged skyward, so that the whole mass was in slow commotion. It had meant death to fly there. When it grew dark, the cloud became alive with lightning, which flickered continuously within it. After dark, the cloud spread far, covering everything and raining.

Soon after our arrival, I stayed rather longer over Anzio than was wise. On my return, a storm-cloud, starting over Gaeta point, barred my passage. I did not have sufficient petrol in the tanks to fly over it, it draped too low on the sea in this mountainous district to fly under it, so I had perforce to fly through it. The manual says that lightning will strike an aircraft only if it carries a trailing aerial. Theory in these circumstances is slight comfort. Bayonets of hail struck against the plane. Up-currents hoisted us, down-currents thrust us down again, ice formed thickly and ominously on the windshield. It was impenetrably dark. For a second the whole cloud was brilliant with lightning, and the wireless crackled and spat, then blindness again and the wild buffeting of the machine. It is uncomfortable having a mountain like Vesuvius in the aerodrome circuit, doubly so when it is erupting. The storm had treacherously reached base, and the bombers which were also flying that night had been recalled. As we broke cloud and came in under low cloud, we found seven or eight of them with their navigation lights on, circling the aerodrome, just above the ground. One end of the aerodrome was open, one end was in torrential rain. Every minute the scene was illumined by lightning, then all was black again, and we slid between mountain, trees and cloud trying to avoid each other in the blue-black darkness. Then there was a flash of another sort, one of the bombers had flown into the ground and exploded. Both Willie and I were glad to land safely.

Then Willie also became sick and was compelled to give up flying. This was sad.

We had for long been enjoying a strange existence, but I could not myself complain, since I had come to despise that unjustifiable criterion, the normal. Our nightly forays could hardly be called ordinary.

From the first, schooling is an attack upon improbability, so that schooling a child, as the name implies, resembles schooling a horse; we render it docile to the bit, and teach it that there are no fauns in the hedge-bottoms. Thence we put the child into uniform; and by regulation enforce uniformity. Thus it is processed; and at the end of the conveyor-belt, comes off a cheap utility man, in a utility suit, both nearly the real thing. Death decimates our number but the ranks of Everyman are filled again. The human atoms combine into fresh molecules of industry; the looms tailor and the presses preach; this is the movement styled 'Continuous Creation'.

The psychologist, the poor man's father-confessor, assists in this, robed in all the metaphysical horror of the ancient seer. The theology of psycho-analysis that appears in tomes printed in America, lays down the heavy values of this profession; and the long technical terms of the modern saints obsess us with their profundity: Dementia Praecox, Libido, Psycho-sexuality, and my particular favourite Furor Uterinus. They point their Forbidding Finger at us in wigged accusation.

Good Christians must desire heaven; should they question this, they are faced with the false alternative, either heaven or hell. All good persons of the scientific age must desire to be conventional; for they are told that they are either the factory-made man or – Dementia Praecox, misplaced Libido, Psycho-sexuality, or Furor Uterinus.

Outside in the country, are not we entertained by gnarled trunks of trees; by puff-balls and salamanders; fleshy fly-catcher leaves; strange pot-holes in rocks? If these can please, why regiment men?

I often wondered whether obeying the law did not undermine character.


## THE NIGHTMARE

I had grown immeasurably tired.
The blue-black of steel, of oerlikon barrel;
out of the blackness, growing apparent, a mirror-image
on polished cannon, the vault of heaven and stars;
the smoky black of smoked glass through which eclipse.
The stars wheel, now not silent, oiled timepieces,
but unoiled,
jangling and jarring as they grind their contrary courses.
I am jelly underneath, a crab without a shell,
lobster with sloughed horn,
cuckoo-spittle, squashed snail, a trod caterpillar,
a fish in the craw of a shark,
a jelly-fish rubbed on a rock,
all brain-tumours, a slob of jelly,
blob, pulse, squinny.

The vast blocks of abrasive meteorite cruising overhead
are not insulated by space
but their unseen weights are rubbing against me,
they swing around,
walls to a drunk and they grind me with pumice.
Tired, tired of never-absent fear,
of effort, tired of perpetual sadness.
I am my legs and my arms and my squelching stomach
and my blood,
an overblown sperm,
amid rock and rock-faces, rock-cliffs, rock-mountains,
rough rock planets, in a rock universe.
I desired to find a rift,
a fault in the rock-face,
where I might slither and hide,
liquid,
who had been fantastically puked up by existence,
wet, sensible, into carborundum.

# Chapter 29

# The Break-Out from Anzio

Willie was replaced by one Wint, a frail flight-sergeant from the Midlands of England. He was characteristic of people from those overcrowded cities in that he was diminished, and when stripped, resembled grass that has long lain under a stone. Also typical of those cities, he possessed the sovereign quality of spirit. I nicknamed him the Shrimp. Then, by divine guidance, I came across a Chinese proverb which ran: 'To become a dragon, a shrimp must pass a most rigid examination.' This I frequently chanted to him and it enraged him beyond measure. When others called him the Shrimp, he would bare his tiny knuckles: 'I don't mind my pilot calling me Shrimp because he's my pilot, but – ' and then he let fly. He developed quickly into a first-class navigator.

The aircrew were now generally inexperienced, undertrained at the squadron level and of indifferent human material. But there were a few excellent exceptions; for instance an able Welsh sergeant, whose name I have forgotten, with a pleasant faun-like navigator; also an Australian, Stewart, who possessed that quiet concentration upon his profession which was the mark of the coming expert. He was maturing when I left the squadron, and had scored a number of successes. Another Australian, Jerry, also flew well. He was a pretty lad, and at the same time he was well up to the high standard of Anzac pilots. I think he worked at a racing-stud before the war. In sum, it was a squadron that lacked the hard nucleus of able pilots, I rather supposed, because the nucleus had been held back in England against the Normandy landings.

At this time there came to us the ancient aviator. He was long past the proper age for our profession; a tanned, crow-footed bachelor; a gnome of a man; addicted to sun-bathing, swimming the crawl and flying – in that order of compulsion. Pop Coleman arrived at a time when the inexperienced pilots were a little shaky. They used to chase the guided bomb instead of the bomber and scuttle if the weather or the German proved unusual. One pilot was chased all the way back to the aerodrome by a permanent blip on his radar set. I hoped that the ancient aviator would bring to us steadiness, for he had been a flying instructor for many years. In the event, he proved almost too steady; for he had reached that time of life when a man has accumulated too great knowledge.

At this date, the break-out from Anzio was planned. The Germans, I believe, ran about six hundred lorries each night through Florence to Rome and the southern supply bases to aid the troops investing the beach-head. Pop Coleman and I were asked to strafe them. There was ample moon but the sky was unfortunately overcast at three thousand feet. This shrouded the roads. The ancient aviator, whose eyesight I think was a little uncertain, failed to see anything.

Wint and I flew along the coastal roads north of Rome. Under the cloud it was bumpy but the moonlight was adequate. The lorries here were close to the fighting, so they wisely dimmed their lights. We had to descend to fifteen hundred feet to see them. The countryside through which we travelled was reasonably flat. We passed Viterbo from where the Popes had once waged war on the great Frederick of Sicily; now, of more importance for us, it held a fighter station. We saw no flying from it. Then we travelled across Umbria to Tuscany. We found and attacked five lorries but we could not see results. The disturbed air made shooting difficult; for as I put the sight onto the target, a bump would throw me off aim, and there was little time in that uncertain light to repair the error. On this strafing trip, I flew under one of my own cannon shells, which ricocheted off the road almost straight into the air.

I spotted a sixth lorry. It appeared to be parked under trees. I hung around, waiting for it to emerge. Its two headlights were burning but it remained where it was. So I decided to attack it there. We dived onto it, the throttles an inch or two open. I fired. As the shells exploded I saw my error. It was no lorry we had noticed but the top storey of a country mansion, with two lights burning in the windows. I pictured to myself the local countess, standing before her mirror shaving herself under her arm, when, wumpf! cannon shells passing through the window splashed into the wall behind.

The following night we were on the last patrol before dawn, and spotted the big cannon which came down by rail from Rome and pitched shells from an immense distance into the harbour. All was quiet elsewhere so we paid it attention. We were not armed with bombs, and it was too dark for us to shoot at it, but the gunners could not know that, so they stopped firing, and fired no more that night. Within a week the break-out occurred. As the Germans left their fox-holes and took to the roads, the day-fighters caught them. Mustangs, Spitfires and Thunderbolts in their packs caught them. When we arrived over the beach-head the length of the road to Rome was marked out by burning vehicles, the fires making a string of lights that reached to the capital.

The night-sky had become complex. A variety of British and American planes were used: Wellingtons, Liberators, Mitchells, Marauders, Halifaxes, Bostons, Beaufighters, Mosquitoes, Marylands and Baltimores. The Germans used French or Italian aircraft in addition to their own types: the Ju 88 and Ju 188, Heinkel 188, Dornier 217, Ju 87, Me 110 and the Me 410: while the Fascist Air Force still operated a squadron of Italian three-engined torpedo-bombers, which were flown with skill. Our job was to identify friend from foe in the darkness. At the time of the break-through, the Luftwaffe used for a day or two every aircraft they could muster for this minor front. It was not many.

That night, as I remember it, was clear with a good moon. I took the second patrol and had no sooner arrived over the beach-head than a raid started. The Germans had been using Ju 87s latterly, because these elderly dive-bombers flew so slowly that Beaufighters overshot them at night. In fact, as we flew up to Anzio, American voices in rich, southern accents had come surprisingly to us on the radio out of the mountains and the darkness promising a bottle of Bourbon whisky to the first Beaufighter crew able to fly slow enough to catch a Stuka. They never paid up. We were put on to a bogey, an unidentified aircraft, and almost immediately I got a visual on a Stuka at six hundred yards range, weaving gently as it flew south. I dropped thirty degrees of flap, slowed down until the great gun-platform was wallowing in the air and then, as the Stuka crossed from starboard to port, fired at about two hundred yards range. One cannon shell exploded near the pilot's seat and the Stuka dived for the ground. I watched it in the milky air. Streams of tracer hurried past me as the gunner, in place of parachuting, fired back. I saw it dive all the way down into the Alban Hills, where it exploded, with a flash that lit the countryside. An aircraft falling away from you thus, when it is moonlight, resembles an object sinking through a well of water.

The control vectored us towards another aircraft. It was again a Ju 87, but fly. For as I caught sight of him at about eight hundred yards, the pilot noticed me. He jettisoned his bombs over his own side of the line and dropped like a stone for the ground. We dived after him, but no Beaufighter could emulate a Stuka at this and he disappeared among the shadowy hills and was gone.

Soon after, ground control gave us a third contact. The Shrimp was working with great skill at the back. The aircraft we were chasing seemed to suspect our presence, for the pilot was diving, twisting and turning, it would seem doing all that he could to elude us. Then he flew straight a minute. We were above the Tiber, at a point where it was small. We closed in and I saw the slender and beautiful form of an Me 110, a German nightfighter, out on the same game as ourselves. I closed in further, raised the nose and fired. There was a moment's pause; two white parachutes opened beneath us like Japanese paper-flowers in a bowl of water; the plane turned onto its back and plunged into the hills.

They gave us a fourth contact, a bandit which knew very well we were after it. I expect the German ground-control had watched proceedings this far. For although we clung to it as it fought for its life, losing it twice and being put back onto it twice, we eventually overshot it – how I do not know. But the Shrimp avers that he looked up and saw the reflection of its exhausts in his cupola. So, in the deteriorating light, we must have nearly rammed it.

Then, petrol being short, we flew home through the dark.

Ground-crews laid side-bets on their pilots, and the cook-house joined in, so if you won the money for the boys, they would ensure you received an extra soya-bean sausage or an additional reconstituted egg for breakfast. For gaming reasons, if for no better, ground-crews would never allow their pilot to be slow off the ground. So we were well fed the next day.

# Chapter 30

# The Landing in the South of France

We used to wonder, at times, what German infantrymen thought of their enemies. For they were motley. On the Italian front there were New Zealanders, both white and Maori; there were Indian troops of many kinds; also Canadians, Goums and Poles; Americans including the American Negro, and the American Japanese. There were South African and many British divisions, Newfoundland artillery, Italian mountain troops and, latterly, Brazilians. Each nation had a style of fighting of its own; and representatives of each were to be found in the crowded cities behind the line.

The British officers' club in Naples contained much of this mixture. All kinds of fighting-men were to be found in its great lounge, with a stiffening of padres. Two Italian ladies sang to them, Fifi and Mimi. Fifi was the only one I ever saw. Her approach was warm and alluvial. She was prepared to sing Lili Marlene all night. As her voice trilled in the enormous room, her middle-aged hands plucked at her skirt as if she were a shy, ten-year-old-girl. Report said, that if she liked you she would sit at your table; and if she really liked you, you were permitted to see her home. But, report said, you must leave early because of the neighbours. She gave you in the morning the door-key; and then lowered into the street from her bedroom window a basket on a string, into which you placed the key, whence it was raised to her room again.

I enjoyed the local comedy although it also brought its difficult moments. For example, about this time I was asked to buy some wine for our mess. The peasant who was offering the wine, suggested to me that I should accompany him to his home in order to sample it. I agreed to this. He had a little cart without sides, consisting of a few planks, a pair of wheels, and one white cow. 'Come here,' he said, 'Jump on.' So I climbed on and lay back.

I had never travelled behind a white cow before. You could feel each precise, delicate movement on the cart. As each white foot was placed on the dusty track exactly where it should be, I mused that a great student of this mode of transport would be able to infer by the lurch of the cart which muscle she was using. The sky above me was amethyst. The fields on either side carried lucerne and bearded wheat. They were shaded by walnut-trees to which vines clung. During the winter the road had been mud; now it had dried to a light, powdery dust. If one had to fight a war, it seemed, what grander place than Italy! I dozed. I heard voices so I raised my head. This fellow's house, I discovered, lay the other side of wing headquarters; and his white cow had borne me, in full uniform, supine through the middle of their camp. It was such small diversions I enjoyed. For small things rather than great carry conviction.

For instance, historians say that after the defeat of the Persians, the luxurious cities opened up to the Greek, and the greater richness of this new world brought enthusiasm for things Persian to such heat that the old veterans of Macedon grumbled to the brink of treachery and revolt. I am this Macedonian. For our latest conquests, in aeronautics, in biology and in physics; for this new man, 'homo aeronauticus', for the globetrotter – as specifically misfeatured as the lily-trotter – I feel some small respect; yet my Cato and conservative half cannot be persuaded that the small patch cultivated at home is not at least as rewarding as the foreign field.

These forced marches across the universe have their parallel in time. For those who have read, who have followed the Decline of Rome with Gibbon, the reported Decline of the West with Spengler, who over the shoulder of Sir James Frazer have studied all witchcraft, there are many pleasant conceits; for they may draw their rule of life from the Toda or the nomes of Akkad; illustrate tea-pot morality with the effete of Ravenna; compare the curate to the indigenous – and now extinct – inhabitants of Tierra del Fuego. To dig down through the layers of anthropology, to compare spokeshave and arrowhead, awl and drill – embedded codices – from the abandoned shelters of the earth, to hobnob with millennia and to quote centimillennia with the same sort of respect as was previously accorded to the aristocracy, is to cite the modern quality. But yet, on all that I turn my back, esteeming Wordsworth's type of the wise who soar but do not roam.

For I am in love with the microscopic as against the macroscopic, the small as against the great, the cool soil of domesticity against political jungles. For at its best, the world is raw material, its size and contours of relative importance. Regarded so, it is raw material for the human spirit. Knowledge is part of a man, much as are his arms and his legs. But the extent of the field over which it has been gathered is of no importance in itself. Your expert on dust and grit, the chronicler of three street corners, the cubic yard eclectic, will make as rich and generous company as a master mariner. The furtively gathered stub can touch the heart, piteous as the massacre of prisoners. The small eddy, the miniature whirlwind that in its passage gathers straw and newspaper, bent matchsticks and the varied dust off the street is the same natural enigma, the same display of the marvellous as the great water-spouts witnessed by the venturesome Voss or the mighty tornado that lifted the warships of Japan, that terrible night, to deposit them in the fields.

Your corner is your seat in the stalls. The Zulu who works upon the curbstone, the urban beachcomber, is advantaged above a box in La Scala. Your ponderous entertainments are for those who lack the sensitivity or the perception to return to the source. He pours from the bottle who cannot draw from the wood. He is no historian whose provenances are avoidably second-hand.

There is not one universe, for owing to the displacement of parallax, each of us inhabits privately his own. To one country there are as many lands as inhabitants. To any continent there are blessed islets whose rock-strewn shores are washed by the traffic of but a single street.

So it seemed to me then. At this time we protected the fleet that bore the Eighth Army to the South of France. It was well north of Corsica when I was guarding it. Nothing special happened.

# Chapter 31

# The Line Reaches Leghorn

As soon as the infantry had broken out of Anzio, we took over the landing-strip there.

That small enclave had previously been filled with anti-aircraft guns at a period in the war when the Allies had been well supplied. As we closed in on a German bomber, Control would say: 'Follow him over the beach-head, we'll hold the guns.' But, quite as often as not, as we raced through the darkness over the harbour, the radio would break in – 'We can't hold them much longer' – and then the ground became brilliant beneath us as every gun let fly. The light flak used tracer; and a strong swarm of crimson balls climbed up to us through the darkness, purposeful as bees, while the less spectacular but more effective shell-bursts of the heavier guns rode beside us out over the Mediterranean as we plunged to safety. Fortunately, neither the British Navy nor the American artillery could shoot, so that the ancient aviator was the only person whose Beaufighter was actually struck. Our own aerodrome defences succeeded in putting three bullets into his aircraft, when he had flaps and wheels down, navigation lights on, and was coming in to land.

But now the beach-head had grown quiet, war had receded north. Nightingales caroled from the bushes and the calm Mediterranean lapped sandy shores. It was already high summer. I found a hive there, a swarm that had been taken by some soldier and placed in a Verey cartridge box. The comb and the Verey cartridges were commingled, two Reds and a Blue, honey, two

Greens and a Red, more honey and so on. So I acquired the bees. And as we moved forward from landing field to landing field, Shrimp wrapped them in a mosquito-net, stowed them in with the guns and flew them with us. We never took honey.

I think that the ants were chiefly responsible. The bees were certainly demoralised by each move, and wasted three or four days to settle down in each new territory. But ants in a long file would shin up a chair-leg, stream past the guard in to the chamber and rifle the honey as fast as the bees collected it. I dressed the chair-legs with old engine oil. But we would be detached to another aerodrome for a day or two, and when we returned, I would find the oil dry and the ants again in the buttery.

Here too I became acquainted with the cicada. To one who had laboured in the closed classroom over 'O fons Bandusiae' and the ancient poet sighing for his lost youth, it was an introduction to a friend's friend. They chirred under the molten sun at midday, while I dozed by a small stream, naked, sleeping off the cares of the previous night.

The meadow where we had encamped was flat and almost on a level with the calm, tideless sea. As it was summer, the grass was dry and sparse with a fair few wild flowers in it. Bathers had only to run barefoot thirty yards over the coarse grass, push through a screen of bushes and they were on the sands.

Soon after our arrival, we were flying near Elba. Corsica had fallen to the Allies some weeks previously. We suspected the Germans to be flying reconnaissance aircraft from the South of France down the west coast of Italy to Naples, and then across to Corsica and back home again. They were supposed to pass through the sector each night, flying low down on the water with the aid of electric altimeters to avoid detection. We had been threading our way through an assortment of our own night bombers, when the ground-control began to direct us after an unidentified aircraft coming south. It was flying low, they said, but they were doubtful of its height.

We made contact with it and the Shrimp brought us in. Then I saw it. It was far below us, black against the moonlit sea, flying just above the water. As we dropped onto it I saw that it carried a tall distinctive tail, either of an Me 410 or a Ju 88. I had thought by strict self-discipline to have cut most part of the risk out of our profession but I was now faced with fighting in the middle of the night just above the waves. He seemed to be cruising at about 250 mph. I judged it essential to avoid a dog-fight, or we should both of us end in the sea, so I closed in fairly fast. He grew big. I could dimly see the waves speeding past just underneath my wing.

The gun-sight is a ring of red light. I had to take my eye off the water and peer through this ring, which though it had been dimmed for night-work, still dazzled. I fired at the Ju 88 and missed. We were now close to him. I fired a long burst again: cannon shells and machine-gun bullets exploded the length of his port wing and engine. He returned the fire, streams of scarlet tracer passing above my starboard wing. He climbed up to six hundred feet and lost speed. I climbed after him but overshot. As I turned in to him, he manoeuvred correctly by turning into me. I passed just above him. I made a wide turn to come in behind him but he had disappeared. At that point ground-control also lost him on their screen, and never saw him again. After studying the plot, we conjectured that he had gone into the water for he was full of lead. Pop Coleman found wreckage, oil, an empty dinghy and fluorescence there the next morning.

The days passed. We went further forward up the west coast, finding the peasant dialects in our new neighbourhoods so different from the south that we had almost to learn another language. We kept to the sea's edge, camping by the water. About this time I had trouble with the bees. It had been a hot afternoon. I was half asleep in the sun, clad only in a bathing-suit, when I noticed that the bees were suffering from the heat, massing just outside the entrance to the hive, fanning the air with their wings. So I scrounged a wooden box with which to make them a false roof and placing it on the hive from behind, met trouble. For they were vexed by this. Italian bees are normally kind, courteous insects, unlike the English bees which I had inherited while I was on 125 Squadron, who were always spoiling for a fight. There, Pat Boyd and I could only handle them in full flying-kit, complete with gas mask. Here I had taken liberties, and except for one occasion when I had been chased in and out of my tent, they had seemed grateful for this care.

Now, however, I was naked. Their note climbed three octaves, and they rose in a cloud into the air, beginning that swift menacing dart from side to side which I had learned to fear. It was fifty yards to the sea. I was compelled, therefore, to stand quite still and pretend to be some dead thing. My body must have smelled of sweat, against which the bee book had warned me, a book that marvellously combined theology with bee-keeping. At last their anger abated and I could step noiselessly away.

A few nights after this the Shrimp and I were above the mountains when we were advised of trade coming south. The Germans had not now many aircraft to spare and were still using the Ju 87 at night, whose very slowness protected it. There was a sliver of a moon. We made contact with an aircraft, and a minute or two later I saw a Ju 87 ahead of me. As we closed in he caught sight of us, thrust his nose down and dived for the protection of the mountain-tops. I pushed my Beaufighter down and opened fire, letting him fly through the pattern. I saw one cannon-shell explode amidships. We waited for a full minute; and then the tell-tale fire broke out below.

We were put after another Ju 87 soon afterwards. We attacked it twice and I think missed it twice – why I did not know. The sight was a moveable one and it may have become unseated; or perhaps I had grown cocksure of my shooting. With the second attack a shell pre-exploded at the muzzle, the flash blinded me for a second and when I could see again, the Stuka was gone.

# Chapter 32

# Return to England

Soon, my tour of operations was complete, and I was posted back to the transit camp at Naples, where I waited for a passage to England. And while waiting, I spent a week or so at the RAF rest camp at Sorrento, sleeping, eating and bathing. The Shrimp must of force stay with the squadron to complete his time. I noticed that my replacement had come out quite quickly, so that I had only exceeded the period of a tour by some thirty operational hours when he arrived. This was fishy. But I only learnt later that my careful mother, as mothers will, had gone to Winston Churchill. And he, great man that he was, had spared her in the middle of the war twenty minutes of his time and had then recalled me personally.

Two or three Italian partisans used to come to the small beach. They wore red shirts, breeches and jack-boots; youths of eighteen and nineteen, with a great swagger for the girls. Especially when they put on bathing-caps before entering the sea in order to preserve the crimp in their hair, the Anglo-Saxons were delighted.

A tall, voluptuous woman passed us one afternoon, kindled by the sun, such a one as Gauguin had painted. The sun had filled her breasts, and tawnied her, a figure of fertility, with paddock value. At her heels trotted two Italian men, small and frail as are that race; so that my companions began to ask whether it was the strength and compliance of Italian women that were responsible for the weakness of their men.

Little girls leapt shrieking into the water from the hewn rocks, and rose to the surface with their brown hair opening to the sea, like petals. For myself, I was weary and could do little but sleep and eat there.

For I think that although night-flying was safer than many forms of Air Force work, it was probably as exacting as any of them. It was more than four years since I had first joined 264 Squadron. For a few pilots, this life comprised all their ambition, and so for them, I believe, it proved less taxing. I had enjoyed to the full the magnificence of flight, I had acquired a taste for it and an aptitude for it, but I remained horrified by its end term. This division did not make my life easier. I enjoyed the chase but I was not reconciled to the kill. I could not become reconciled to the kill. It was hard, too, to look after friends. Every pilot came to know that sudden black cloud of smoke, which told of burning oil, a crashed aircraft, dead or mutilated crew.

Fatigue can of itself bring a sort of understanding. The shaking hand, the irregular heartbeat, unnecessary bleeding, and for a day or two an alarming state of blindness, both indoors and out, made me conscious of the versatility of a person. For I could find, stirring within me, strange possibilities.

With ideas we can be out of sympathy with but few people. There are those who say: 'I cannot understand how he came to do it.' Yet a little thought and we so often can. For as every nation carries representatives of each human type, so each of us carries a nation inside him. Who is not sharp with his inhabitants and morally arbitrary, in this a low churchman, will possess a nodding acquaintance with half the world. He will know how Himmler came to be, or Helen, or a cockney trooper, or the Lord of Belsen. He may not support what they do or have done, but he will have felt the fires of creation quicken; or he will have made the excuse, essayed the self-deception; even as the paragons of evil have made it.

But it is not with contemporaries only that we sympathise. The actions and outlook of men two, four and six millennia ago, when we know of them, seem strangely familiar and in time. Lack of data parts us as far from a modern man as from an ancient; through ignorance I am further separated from the native Mayor of Papua than from Sappho; from the present Cham than from Naboth; from the Akond than from Akhnaton. I could observe with Strabo, and massacre with Eichmann: I could whore and rise to an empery with Theodora and be strangely compassionate with Las Casas. If we acquaint ourselves with their actions, do we not number them among our peoples, able to call upon their strength and their weakness, able to summon them from among the citizens to be mayor of ourselves?

So deeply in touch with oneself, therefore, gives understanding, with the negress shrill-singing by the Nile, and the old peasant sleeping in the ruins of his German home.

One is led, insistently, to ask what makes these wars, that hang on from old times, but to my eyes appeared bizarre and old-fashioned? We could fly over a nation in an hour. The rhetoric of their politicians seems to be quite out of touch with modern needs. They repeat the angry passages of an earlier world. The present questions which are live and quick, they ignore. Scarlet uniforms, tanks, War Ministries, the paraphernalia of the embattled nation-state, are really very odd.

There are many causes of war. But it seems to me that corrupted scholars and young men are dangerous. In part, it is the unexploded young men. For husky youths, fed, wormed and restrained are offered inadequate adventure. So that though the causes of war be diverse and though the machinery of international government and co-operation be inadequate, yet also the dishonesty of intellectuals and the pettiness of urban existence prepare the way for the explosion of the young men. We have imprisoned ourselves behind imaginary barriers because we fear to see the Pacific of possibility by which we are surrounded. We are afraid of our own freedom. We have pondered too little upon it.

Rather must we maintain our liberties, enriching our minds with outlooks that have not before been acceptable, returning to the goals of the idealist philosophers in contemporary dress – the headlong pursuit of beauty in all its forms, the pursuit of knowledge for the dignity it brings to the human condition beyond any commercial use that can be made of it, the idea of virtue as being a personal ethic as new and creative as a pure mathematic.

# Chapter 33

# The End

I arrived gratefully in London, burning my Mediterranean uniform because it had grown too dilapidated to be cleaned. After a fortnight's leave, I received a telegram to report to the Air Ministry's Manpower Research Unit at Marston Moor in Yorkshire. I hesitated whether I was to be a subject or object of research, until I arrived at that bleak aerodrome, where I found myself in charge of a small RAF party which sought, along with civilians and with other groups, to rationalise the organisation and administration of Bomber Command. I guessed that this was given me because of my slender acquaintance with economics. It was original work, and I learned much by it. A neat Alan Philpotts, back in England after his Wooden Horse escape, was at the Whitehall end of this inquiry.

Life was very peaceful. Between the hours when we attempted to get most bombs out of the heavy bomber force, whose limiting factor was a shortage of ground-crew, I took to studying the nature of Evil; not, after all, an unrelated study. Furthermore, it seemed to me that negative ethics might be more revealing than positive. David Hume has observed that in England the obscurer sciences are studied with especial zeal. Yet even there, the science of Evil has gone neglected; since those who wish to be its students dare not; and when they stumble upon a fragment of its primer, they fear to name it. Socrates was notorious for saying that Evil was a kind of ignorance; believing perhaps, that since Evil was not studiously pursued it was not studiously pursuable. There will soon come, I prophesy, a great shag-headed genius, a man who is mature, evolved, ready to pursue Evil with that knowledgeable insistence the industrialist dotes upon his trade.

For great evil and great poetry are at present the creation of genius; ill-doing springs from the wild wood-notes of malice. Genius lights truth, science formulates it, the common man uses it. Negative ethics seeks to put this study on a proper footing, with clear principles, so that progress may be made in it. For there has been little constructive thought about Evil since the great days of the Persians. Many works come off the University presses upon the Right and the Good, gelded because they study but the half of their subject; as if a man studying physics were to weigh heat and not cold; or a geographer so dwell upon his hemisphere he refuse countenance to his Antipodes. I want a Chair of Evil, a College of Ill-doers, bursaries for subtle destruction.

The study is partly experimental. We may take a hint from the Christian writer Hippolytus who defines the Devil as 'he who resists the cosmic process'. This process is reported to be a movement towards Virtue, Beauty and Knowledge. Devotees are drawn thither by an inner instinct working among the facts of their existence. It is a portion of the Universe becoming self-conscious and harkening to its own compulsion. If you break open a human termitary and kick the parts of it to fragments, the small survivors, after a period of frustration, will gather themselves again and commence to build once more. They build according to the necessities of their material and their own inner light, however little they know what they do. The elected mayor exhorts them to their duty, the medalled patriot emphasises that their duty is important, the termitary statesman explains that no other termitary in this camp would have recovered so fast; the females, the guardians of the termitary instincts, ensure that the workers build according to set plan by assailing them, should they deviate, with the increased excitement of horror. The greatest and most sensitive termites, the artists, build representations of how this inner light appears to them in order to inspire the workers. They tell little stories of how it may be built in other ways, thus suggesting to the more silly worker what is possible for him to achieve. We are not fooled as are ants. For although taboo and habit, and the strict censor in the head which suppresses unfair questions even before they are raised, govern our termitaries rigidly, our habits are slowly modified and relaxed by eccentrics and artists. Thus, after many mistakes, our kind of termite builds a little better each year, and in this way modifies himself towards that pattern which the artist and seer suggest to him.

Evil, then, is to resist this process; to refuse to accept that inner harmony, creativeness and compulsion. It is normally trivial. But careful study should suggest a better course, a disciplined coherent movement to a self-appointed end among the interstellar spaces, generating private satisfactions and delights.

For Evil rewards study. It should not be left to the advice of historians, those old wives of immorality. That which is physically harmful is already studied; death is normally its end term. The purest evil lives, it is a condition of the mind. In the lowest kingdoms of triviality it is found: fostering the plain, the ugly, the petty, the church-goer's morality, the mediocre, the box-office of democracy. It overcomes important men. God tolerated Satan; both Bible Spirits prospered by religion.

Milton, in steel and concrete paragraphs, depicted Evil; not as licentious, ill-disciplined, cruel; not as Evil appears in the outer palaces and keeps, but as he is in the Sanctuary; noble, resolute, defiant. The music is present; love is the desire of beauty; the fallen angel is in revolt, intelligent, knowing what he forgoes, leading his cohort in conscious opposition, informed, sensitive, heroic.

Our minds remain traditional. We peep out through Egyptian windows onto the contemporary world. We are in the post-Babylonian period of history. We see history as finite with a near beginning and an end. Life is confined to one plant and a short time. Good and Evil are absolutes, they war for the immortal souls. Theft, perjury and fornication are still held to be cardinal errors.

The genius in Evil will take the facts as statistical examination shows them; he will know the chords that respond; he will know all the dark corners of appetite and suffering. He will then take these facts. And backed by a cartel of contemporary knowledge, he will weave a new and original pattern in Evil, unsubservient to his predecessors, daring and imaginative. A new beauty will emerge, a new ugliness.

A society is the working out of the possibilities in living that may be deduced from a given set of premises expressed in custom and law. The presuppositions of Hell are as important as those of Heaven. We may find, when we have built a coherent system of hate and evil, something more strangely beautiful than that of love; more challenging and more lonely.

In this direction my own inquiry moved. Our more orthodox research into the workings of Bomber Command was of the same order; for as we were concerned how to drop more bombs from a limited bomber force, we sought to blast many more lives. The Royal Air Force had expanded overnight. It was much in need of this sort of introspection and many quaint practices were found.

Of the million or more people in the Royal Air Force, there could have been few, be they never so senior, who had not groaned at some period under the weight of needless paperwork by which life was encumbered. Of all this million, it fell to me, to me only, to initiate a unit of the Air Ministry whose function was to simplify or eradicate bumph. For three revengeful months, the unit travelled from Ministry to the Commands, from Command to Group, from Group to Station, from Station to Squadron, inquiring by whom this form-filling was needed. We soon discovered that there were many bodies whose function was to initiate new forms, none to suppress old and no longer necessary ones. Forms which had been useful in 1941 only, were still being filled in 1944 and 1945, gravely collected, gravely sorted and finally laid to their last rest in some Air Ministry cellar. I have since conjectured that in every state there should be two legislative bodies; one to make new and useful laws, a second to abolish old ones. And the ablest brains should sit in the latter.

Also, we inquired why postings of staff should occur pointlessly, to discover eventually that the Records Office, Gloucester, was run by Air Commodore Cordingley, who refused to allow us into his department to investigate it. We thus discovered that when Major Trenchard had formed the RFC, Sergeant-Major Cordingley had been in charge of his orderly-room. As the RFC grew in size, later to become the RAF, Cordingley advanced in rank, so that in the early months of 1945, no one else save Cordingley had ever been in charge of Air Force postings – and there the matter stood. And little did we know then, a fact which came to light later, that a group of his frustrated clerks were playing 'happy family' with the RAF, shifting people about the world in an endeavour to achieve, with the aid of their minutely detailed reference books, one unit composed entirely of people with scars on the left thigh and another unit composed entirely of people with hare-lips.

When my period of rest was finished, the war was over. So I endeavoured to sell to Lord Cherwell, back in Christ Church, the opinion that there was a sovereign equation, for the Royal Air Force in peace-time as for a national economy, whose factors could be discovered, which would proportion that part of the total income to be spent upon research, that part upon the application of this research and that part upon day-to-day living. He was voted out of office with Winston Churchill before I could make progress. I remained with the Air Ministry a little while longer; and then, just before leaving the Air Force upon demobilisation, I was given command of a ferrying unit which was already disbanded. I succeeded in keeping it going a further month, while we helped to tidy up Europe of its warplanes that were scattered across the continent. Outside our dispersal hut was ranged a line of pleasant aircraft: Tempests, Typhoons, Mustangs, Spitfires, and twin-engined aircraft, Wellingtons, Marauders, Mosquitoes, Mitchells. With them I had my last delightful fling. Each type had its separate, nostalgic smell. We now stand, Tartars without horses.

But so we got to Eindhoven and Bückeberg, Brussels, Lübeck and Copenhagen before our last mechanic was posted from underneath us. From the air, I surveyed the cities of Western Germany, that were ruin and broken by that aerial artillery which was created in the days we won for it. I was astonished, reviewing Hamburg, to see that so many bombcraters fitted into so confined an area. The harbour carried only upturned ships or funnels queerly appearing through the water. Yet the streets of rubble were black with people. Our long night vigils on the aerial walls of Britain had availed nothing, it had often seemed to us at the time. But the factories beneath us, blast furnaces concealed, were in fact working night and day to produce the crawling tanks and the armoured cars, the bombers and the landing-craft, which properly used, had ground to powder Nazi Germany and all her bestial ambitions.

# Chapter 34

# The Substitute for War

The day came to be demobilised. I had never been bold enough to dare believe I should live. Now they gave me my gents' suiting, including a cloth cap which my great-aunt Doods wore with distinction, and I walked the streets again, a free man. When we met our fellows, we discussed survivors, like two pheasants at the season's close.

At the beginning it felt a little odd. It seemed, at the age of twenty-six, as if I had been through the whole range of human experience and had lived out one life entire. For into six months of active flying a pilot compressed the emotional experience of a lifetime.

I grew fit again, for I left the Air Force feeling twisted, out of place, bitterly mis-shapen.

My octogenarian great-aunt helped in this recovery. She was a lady who had style, a relic of the previous century, dwelling in a large Victorian house, chock-a-block with furniture. Her life had found its moorings and its fulfilment in the Cottesmore hunting country; so that now, by short-sightedness rather than frailty denied that which gave her life meaning, she stayed cheerfully at home, chopping wood in the garden, reading the horoscope in the papers, or lunching on a Sunday with other gentlefolk of a similar age. 'They tell me they had a capital hunt on Tuesday, but the new Master, they say, he can't hunt hounds and he will persist in hunting them.' Her house was full of paintings, all of which depicted horses. Her lame butler, at least as old as she, used to invite me to dine with her. She had a stick of paratroopers billeted there, who found her, they said, something tougher than themselves.

On my demobilisation leave I returned to Oxford where I became a sort of undergraduate again. The old routine remained. Beneath her bells the medieval life continued in the narrow streets and I had leisure to browse in the great libraries, for whose pastures I had yearned. There were the same sort of undergraduates there as when I left, the Aesthetes, the Blue-Bloods, the Scholars. I rejoined the Air Squadron, in order to eat a square meal again. As I stepped into the ante-room, a ruddy-faced instructor called Tiger David, with an enormous handlebar moustache, was speaking. The first words I heard from him were: 'Tempests in Baluchistan.'

Alan Howe remained the gamekeeper at Bletchington. The partridge shooting, he told me, had improved, since much of the grass had been ploughed. His eldest son had been killed in Libya with the artillery. His two younger sons had landed in Normandy as Tank Commanders. Now they were home again, and happy to be out of the services.

One quiet evening I was strolling with a friend through the green lanes near Sutton Courtenay, in that fertile Thames countryside, when we lit upon a war-memorial raised to the memory of one man. There are scarce five houses in the village. Thinking on it, I was led to believe that our opinions about war had subtly changed, and that this widespread erection of crosses, monoliths and tablets, with those lying words carved upon them, 'Their Names Liveth for Evermore', marked this change. It is a recent fashion; earlier, men had wished their souls, not their names, to be preserved.

Yet it is not so much that we have to die that permeates our existence with mystery, it is that we can kill, that it is within our power to destroy other people, to pull down their temples.

We raise these stones, it seems, because men no longer believe it proper to fight. They recognise that in asking a youth to volunteer, they are making extraordinary demands on him. No wonder; for there are limitations to art; synthetic terror is not real terror. It may be that in earlier periods soldiers believed themselves to pass on to their reward. The aircrew I knew were largely atheist. But at times men think. Some of them will believe, as I believed, that though it was needful to fight, what we did was also terribly wrong. And that the coming end was not a temporary forgetfulness, or a translation to another state, but absolute destruction, annihilation, nothingness. Their whole universe, as Lucretius describes it, will fall in with a mighty crash. The thought of that near-annihilation for a time casts a cloud, as a pilot, returning at dawn, can change day into night by descending twenty thousand feet.

We ask today of a conscript something more than we were wont to ask of him. I dare believe that these are not new considerations; it is only that more of us amateurs understand it thus. So afterwards we appoint playing fields for children; for frequently, the more likely a man is to be hurt, the more moral he becomes.

Progress comes by substitution. To replace war, we require not only better systems for controlling our politicians – often a crude and irresponsible breed of men – but alternative ways for youth to test itself. War has been for the West almost its puberty ceremony, whose rigours few young men survived, and those who came through had burnt up half their life. Youth wishes to give as much as to be given things; that which was once the monk is now a soldier; tomorrow there must be some other way, for the ordinary man as well as for the dedicated. From the sadness and the cruelty that made up this experience, the oustanding impression left upon me, oddly enough, was the simple goodness of my fellows. The desires of men are clearly noble as well as being very base. Philosophies rest upon them, otherwise they spin through space, foundationless as the earth itself.

I feel strongly that there must be many lessons to be learnt from this war and I feel that there is great urgency that we learn them, but precisely what these lessons should be, puzzles me.

Clearly, more people are prepared to die for their country in wartime than will live for it in peace-time. The abhorrent wastage of war is exceeded in peace. Children in poor countries die of starvation by the million, while armies in rich countries are fed men and guns to defend them against other rich countries.

War and Peace are not separate existences. Wars are made in peace-time and peace shaped and justified out of the harvesting of war. The carnage of one is more spectacular than the other but in the poorer countries there is not much to choose.

In addition, we must never forget that the Germans were the best educated nation in Europe. The savage state into which they sank tells us something very important about all human beings and about ourselves. Evidently mankind must be disarmed of ultimate weapons or some day, some place, it will be unwise enough to use them. This is the lesson from which we may not flinch. Nor, paradoxically, may we yet trust ourselves to a world government or we may be ourselves helpless before a dictatorship of even more curious brutality.

It is widely accepted that men should be careful about claiming that they are poets or artists, because the claim is so big as to suggest arrogance. Yet they will without compunction claim that they are civilised and falsely compare the highly civilised nations of Western Europe to the barbarous African. These recent wars suggest that the word 'civilised' has to be used with equal reserve.

Let us substitute for war a much freer existence in peace-time, directed to developing the empire, not of territory, but of emotional experience and of the mind. Once released from the bridle of convention, it is open to us to cultivate beauty, not only in the fine arts and architecture but also in original dances and sports. Youth should have the world to choose from for its brides. Art is the Reserve Bank of intellect.

Our opportunities, imaginably greater than anything so far

realised, will strain to the limit our human resources. To pick that sword out of the ground, requires the peace-time skills of all nations; each one, by virtue of its different manners, contributing to and helping the other.

In these ways, youth can be given an equal sense of purpose, in peace as in war, and the fatuous and horrifying brutality of the second can be avoided, perhaps for ever.

With some such train of thought, Isaac Newton commented, the apple notwithstanding: 'I do not know what I may appear to the world, but to myself I seem to have been only a boy playing on the sea-shore, and directing myself in now and then finding a smoother pebble or a prettier shell than ordinary, whilst the great Ocean of Truth lay all undiscovered before me.'